REDEFINING BLACK POWER

REDEFINING BLACK POWER

Reflections on the State of Black America

Edited by Joanne Griffith

Open Media Series • City Lights Books
San Francisco

Cover art by Keba Konte

The Open Media Series is edited by Greg Ruggiero and archived by the Tamiment Library, New York University.

 **Pacifica Radio Archives** *A Living History* The interviews for this book were made possible by the generous support of the Pacifica Radio Archives.

eISBN 978-0-87286-548-8 (ebook)

Library of Congress Cataloging-in-Publication Data
Redefining Black power : reflections on the state of Black America / edited by Joanne Griffith.
    p. cm. — (Open media series)
    ISBN 978-0-87286-546-4 (paperback)
1. African Americans—Social conditions—21st century. 2. African Americans—Politics and government—21st century. 3. Obama, Barack. 4. United States—Race relations—21st century. 5. United States—Politics and government—2009– 6. Griffith, Joanne—Interviews. I. Griffith, Joanne.

E185.86.R378 2012
305.896'073—dc23

    2011045459

City Lights Books are published at the City Lights Bookstore, 261 Columbus Avenue, San Francisco, CA 94133.
www.citylights.com

MIX
Paper from responsible sources
FSC
www.fsc.org   FSC® C011935

CONTENTS

Foreword   7
Brian DeShazor

Introduction   11
Joanne Griffith

1 The Movement for the Expansion and
  Deepening of Democracy in America   25
  *A Conversation of Context with Dr. Vincent
  Harding*

2 What about the Brother at the Bottom
  of the Well?   45
  *Law in the Age of Obama with Professor
  Michelle Alexander*

3 Dollars and Sense? Race, Recession,
  and Recovery   71
  *Racial equality and economic parity with
  Dr. Julianne Malveaux*

4 Barack Obama: The New Crack?   93
  A Story of Revolution with Ramona Africa

5 Probing the President: The Media's
  Paralysis of Analysis?   115
  *Race, the Press, and the White House with Linn
  Washington Jr.*

6 It Matters What Needs to Be Done   141
  Politics and Green Activism with Van Jones

7 A Quiet Victory for Emotional Justice   165
   The First Family and the African American
   Psyche with Esther Armah

   Going Forward   187
   Joanne Giffith

   Acknowledgments   191

   Notes   195

   Selected Bibliography and Audio References   199

   About the Editor   203

   About the Contributors   203

FOREWORD

My work is a never-ending history lesson. Every day I learn something new from the thousand's of whispers that cry out from the vault of the Pacifica Radio Archives, a unique collection that is virtually unknown to most Americans, including scholars, educators, and social justice advocates. Over the last decade, it has been my personal goal to see the awe-inspiring words, ideas, experiences, and historic moments documented by the Pacifica radio network become more accessible by way of the written page. This book and the Redefining Black Power: Reflections on the State of Black America project is the beginning of this process.

The idea of a book struck like a lightning bolt while I was listening to a single recording from the vast Pacifica Radio Archives collection.

At the time, I was unfamiliar with Fannie Lou Hamer. Her story is one I hadn't been taught in school. Her voice was like nothing I'd ever heard before. Broadcast from a small studio above an ice cream store on University Avenue in Berkeley was the voice of this woman telling a white, albeit sympathetic interviewer, Colin Edwards, about her work for African American voting rights and her leadership role in the Mississippi Freedom Democratic Party.

Her tone was soft and gentle with its Mississippi drawl and colloquial phrasing, yet it sparked with determination. It was like the heartbreaking voice of Billie Holiday singing "Strange Fruit," but there was no sadness in it, just direct, brutal honesty. I heard the pain and promise of the civil rights movement in those headphones. Her words cut like a dagger as she described the horrific beating she endured—on the orders of a prison guard, two black inmates struck Fannie Lou Hamer with weapons, leaving her blind in one eye. Of one of the men she said, "He beat me until he was exhausted." Sitting alone, the dam of my emotions broke there in the corner of a modest office. This interview has never been transcribed or published. Nor have countless others like it.

There has been a decades-long relationship between Pacifica station KPFA in Berkeley, California, and City Lights Books. In a 2003 interview, City Lights co-founder Lawrence Ferlinghetti recalled reading his poetry for the station in the early 1950s and having to later transcribe a poem from the tape because he had lost his printed copy. This conversation led me to City Lights Books publisher Elaine Katzenberger and editor Greg Ruggiero. Telling them the story about Fannie Lou Hamer and other watershed moments listening to Rosa Parks, James Baldwin, and Angela Y. Davis brought us together on this venture to realize the dream of preserving and sharing these extraordinary voices and adding to the conversation on the current chapter in America's journey with its first black president.

Just as the voices from the black freedom movement held in the archives set the framework for conversations on contemporary African American society today, so I hope this book will open the door to address the many questions raised during the Obama presidency. How will the presence of a black man in the White House change how we talk about and tackle race and racism? How will the media's images of African Americans evolve? What impact will the First Lady, Michelle Obama, have on the psyche of African American women? What role will this historic moment play in the advancement of black America? And around the globe, how will the Obama years shape the way the world views the people of the United States?

This is not the space for answers; delve into the pages of this book to see how contributors responded to these and other questions posed by international journalist Joanne Griffith. Since 2007, following a chance visit to the archives, Joanne has championed the Pacifica Radio Archives, sharing the treasure trove of material on BBC Radio 5 Live's *Up All Night* program, enlightening a new audience to the voices of the well know and the anonymous.

Over the years I've watched Joanne use her journalistic skill and insight to draw out information that we can all digest and discuss. With warmth, she listens loudly and interviews with insight and curiosity, bringing her global sensibility, passion for politics, and heart for the black freedom movement to every conversation. Joanne's work is centered on one theme: not to offer information as a point of journalistic fact, but to act as a conduit for debate and conversation, especially around issues relating to the African diaspora experience. Joanne's work on *Redefining Black Power: Reflections on the State of Black America* is no different. It brings together critical thinking, diverse opinions, and thought-provoking ideas and perspectives often left out of the mainstream conversation, brilliantly reflecting Pacifica's mission of lasting understanding of the human condition and conflict resolution through dialogue.

Thank you for heeding the call of the voices of history. Digest. Discuss. Share. Speak out. Act.

Brian DeShazor
Director of the Pacifica Radio Archives

INTRODUCTION

Before it actually happened, many people thought they'd never live to see an African American command the White House as president of the United States. For generations who dared to even entertain the idea, it was a dream unfulfilled.

The successful campaign and election of Barack Hussein Obama in November 2008 marked a milestone in America's history. A past stained by slavery, discrimination, inequality, genocide, and violence made it difficult to hold out hope that a person could run for office in the United States and not "be judged by the color of their skin but by the content of their character."

Stepping into the political bear pit of the 2008 presidential campaign, then–Senator Obama ignited a fire under people of all races with a simple idea: that the future of the United States could be bigger, brighter, better through hope and change. For people of color and African Americans specifically, it was a longed-for chance to level the playing field; an opportunity to seize their agency and elect a man to power with whom they experienced a profound affinity.

Figures from the Bureau of the Census speak to this political stirring and the importance of Obama's candidacy for black America. For the first time, the historic gap between black and white voter participation narrowed to just 4 percent. The number of African American voters aged eighteen to twenty-four increased by 8 percent from the 2004 presidential election; and in states such as Maryland, South Carolina, Nevada, Ohio, and Mississippi, black voter participation reached 70 percent; the national average for African Americans was 65 percent, compared to 60 percent in 2004.[1] Obama mobilized black Americans like few candidates before him.

Just as with other key moments in political history relating to leaders like John F. Kennedy, Dr. Martin Luther King Jr., and Malcolm X, people remember clearly where they were when Senator Obama became President-elect Obama. I was at home in the stillness of my apartment in Los Angeles, my husband and I glued to the television screen, hoping for the best but expecting the worst; four years of John McCain and Sarah Palin.

As we clicked between election coverage on various TV stations, seeking further confirmation of the result delivered to us by Charlie Gibson, the telephone stirred to life as news of the historic result pulsed around the world and filtered back to Los Angeles. Family and friends in the United States, London, Barbados, and Africa screamed with shock and disbelief, repeating the refrain "did he *really* win?" Barack Obama said "Yes we can," and on November 4, 2008, *we did.*

By the night of Obama's victory, I had been in the United States for a little over a year, a journalist transplanted from London to Los Angeles. Being so close to the action as the campaign unfolded was a dream for a politics major who inhaled news—attending campaign rallies, speaking with community organizers, even spending a day following a celebrity around Los Angeles ahead of the Obama/Clinton rally at the

Kodak Theatre—I devoured it all. Like so many other black people around the world, I felt that I could "claim" Obama politically, whether or not I was a citizen of the United States. Having followed Obama since the 2004 Democratic National Convention only compounded that sense.

For millions of people around the planet, witnessing a black man win the U.S. presidency and command the White House is profoundly powerful. Given the long history of racist enslavement and terrorism in the United States, the very fact that a black man and his black wife and black children live in the most famous house in America is in itself historically transformative. The history books have yet to be written, but President Obama will be judged on the content of his actions, not his family ancestry.

The work of building Obama's presidential legacy began in January 2009; the eyes of the world focused sharply upon him. How would he transform inspirational rhetoric and over five hundred campaign promises into workable policies while tackling the behemoth of an inherited 1.3-trillion-dollar budget deficit, two overseas wars, and a national unemployment rate of 7.6 percent?

President Obama has answered critics with a number of policy successes in his first term to date: the signing of the Ledbetter law, requiring equal pay for women; the creation of new financial regulations; the signing of the universal health care bill; and lethal hits on Al Qaeda's leadership.

There are, of course, promises that have been broken or remain works in progress, including the closure of Guantánamo Bay, a full removal of U.S. troops from Iraq and Afghanistan, a repeal of the Bush-era tax cuts for the wealthy, and increasing the minimum wage to $9.50 per hour.[2]

However, jump-starting the economy and creating jobs have bedeviled the Obama administration. According to the Bureau of the Census, the percentage of Americans living in poverty in 2010 rose to the highest level in seventeen years, while median incomes for the middle class fell by 2.3 percent to under fifty thousand dollars a year.[3] Furthermore, in August 2011, the number of unemployed African American men reached 16.7 percent, double that for white males. For black youth, unemployment hit the astonishing level of 46.5 percent.[4]

"There are roughly 3 million African Americans out of work today, a number nearly equal to the entire population of Iowa," said Democratic Representative Maxine Waters of California. "I would suggest that if the entire population of Iowa, a key state on the electoral map and a place that served as a stop on the president's jobs bus tour were unemployed, they would . . . be the beneficiary of targeted public policy."[5]

After months spent battling with a Republican-controlled Congress over the debt crisis, in late summer 2011 President Obama finally turned his attention to jobs. Speaking before a joint session of Congress, he outlined his 447 billion dollar economic rejuvenation plan:

> The purpose of the American Jobs Act is simple: to put more people back to work and more money in the pockets of those who are working. It will create more jobs for construction workers, more jobs for teachers, more jobs for veterans, and more jobs for the long-term unemployed. It will provide a tax break for companies who hire new workers, and it will cut payroll taxes in half for every working

American and every small business. It will provide a jolt to an economy that has stalled, and give companies confidence that if they invest and hire, there will be customers for their products and services.

From the outset of the speech, President Obama acknowledged that for the millions of jobless Americans, their situation was further magnified by "a political crisis that's made things worse." Yet for those hit the hardest, namely African Americans, there was no specific mention of how they would be helped. Looking ahead, Representative Maxine Waters warns of the damage this could cause the president in 2012: "If the unemployment rates in the African American Community continue to climb . . . those African American voters who came out to the polls for the first time in 2008 but who have since lost their home and/or their job, may not return to the polls."[6]

Although Representative Waters does not view Obama as a president who should privilege the needs of African Americans over those of others, if under the Obama administration Washington does not acknowledge long-ignored issues faced by black America, will it ever? Will President Obama take leadership to shed light on chronic disparities in education, criminal justice, and wealth experienced in black communities? Can the Obamas as a black family, the first African American First Family, uplift the perceptions of people of color in U.S. society? What connections and continuities exist between the present moment and past generations of black freedom struggle? Now that Martin Luther King's statue is part of the canon of official national heroes, how has the very notion of black power changed since he addressed the world from the steps of the Lincoln Memorial, a black man at the front of a historic freedom movement?

These are some of the questions the Redefining Black Power project seeks to explore.

The concept for *Redefining Black Power* was born within the vaults of the Pacifica Radio Archives based in Los Angeles and borrows its name from a *Defining Black Power* program produced by the archives. More than 55,000 recordings are held in an unassuming, climate-controlled room, rows of white cardboard cases with blue marker reference numbers lining every available shelf.

When the director of the Pacifica Radio Archives, Brian DeShazor, approached me with the idea for the *Redefining Black Power* project, his vision was clear: to honor the men and women, families, and youth who drove the black freedom movements, so that their momentous work would be remembered in tandem with, and not eclipsed by, the political, social, cultural forces that gave rise to the Obamas.

Introduced to the Pacifica Radio Archives in 2007, I began to host a weekly show in the United Kingdom using material held in Pacifica's vaults; sharing, among other things, stories of African American struggle and triumph with a whole new audience. The pleas of the well known and the anonymous reach out from the black freedom movement's many areas of vision, advocacy, engagement, confrontation, and struggle: Rosa Parks, Fannie Lou Hamer, Malcolm X, Martin Luther King Jr., James Baldwin, Bayard Rustin, Angela Y. Davis, Kathleen Cleaver, Elaine Brown, Stokely Carmichael, Ossie Davis, Ruby Dee, Lorraine Hansberry, Paul Robeson, Muhammad Ali, Shirley Chisholm, Jesse Jackson, and so many others. Their contributions defined a generation and built the foundation upon which the Obamas and all black Americans now stand. As a popular text that circulated during the 2008 election said:

> Rosa sat so Martin could walk.
> Martin walked so Obama could run.
> Obama is running so our children can fly.

Just as the Pacifica Radio Archives serves as a portal to the past for those who wish to listen and learn from the people who defined a movement, *Redefining Black Power* aims to contextualize and connect the present to past struggle and offer the future an African American narrative on the Obama years.

Redefining Black Power is a work in progress, a wheel in motion made of many spokes—this book, a multimedia Web site, a series of radio programs, and ongoing community conversations and roundtables that address and respond to the changing political moment. During the first six months of the Obama presidency, hosts and producers across the Pacifica Radio network gathered the early thoughts of community organizers, activists, artists, religious leaders, academics, educators, and youth in a series of roundtable discussions and listener phone ins. Conversations anchored by Margaret Prescod, Lucia Chappelle, Aimee Allison, and Gloria Minnott spanned the gamut of campaign memories, election night highs, inauguration day hopes and concerns surrounding the term "post racial."

"I'm a little afraid that I don't understand or agree with the interpretation of the post-racial identity that has come about as a result of the election of Barack Obama," said Karen

Spellman, a Washington DC–based former worker with SNCC, the Student Nonviolent Coordinating Committee. "I think that we, African Americans, have to define when we've reached the end of racism. I don't think that it's incumbent upon those who are the oppressors to tell us we no longer have race as a factor."

As well as sharing their thoughts on the Obama White House, roundtable participants responded to issues dominating the news agenda, including Attorney General Eric Holder's February 2009 speech in which he said, "Though this nation has proudly thought of itself as an ethnic melting pot, in things racial we have always been and continue to be, in too many ways, essentially a nation of cowards."

"I really don't think that Obama's racial makeup and discussions around race should have anything to do with one another," said Mayra Jimenez, who sat on the Youth Panel held at KPFK in Los Angeles. "What he's going to do for the country is one thing; his ethnicity and background are another."

Eric Holder's comments on race were viewed differently by Oakland-based arts activist Marc Bamuthi Joseph: "There is a signpost in the presidency of Barack Obama that points folks of all races into a conversation on race. Now, whether that conversation is a cursory one or whether it leads to widespread transformation is a whole other thing."

In addition to a series of roundtables at the community level, over a two-year period I conducted a series of in-depth conversations with noted scholars, revolutionaries, organizers, authors, and activists representing several generations of progressive black intellectuals. Michelle Alexander, the author of *The New Jim Crow*, sheds light on the criminal justice system and the impact of mass incarceration on African American communities, while economist and Bennett College president Dr. Julianne Malveaux calls for targeted assistance to address rising levels of long-term unemployment within black communities. During our conversation Malveaux insists that if black America wants more, they need to demand more from their leaders and the Obama administration. "The relationship between President Obama and the black community reveals the weaknesses in African American leadership. You don't see the same thing with the gay and lesbian community or with the Latino community. People are going and asking for what they want and they're clear about it. African Americans are not doing that."

For Van Jones, founder of Rebuild the Dream and the former White House Green Jobs adviser, black civic leadership, not elected officials or President Obama, directly address the needs of black America: "it's the NAACP's job to deal with the question of black leadership. It's the Urban League's job, Al Sharpton's job. It's not the president's job. It's not his job to fix black America."

One issue that influences and threads through all of the discussions is the media; from political campaigns to how the Obama girls wear their hair, the media is ever present, and what it chooses to show and not show, and how, directly influences public consciousness and the national narrative itself.

"One of the problems that I see with the American media and the Obama presidency is that the rise of President Obama runs parallel to the continuing decline in the press," explains veteran journalist and *Philadelphia Tribune* columnist Linn Washington. "We have more shallow and sensationalistic coverage versus more probative coverage. On the campaign trail, there were numerous examples of a glaring lack of in-depth coverage, and I think that helped him in some ways, but further polluted the coverage as it affected the deep and insidious issue of race in America."

While *Redefining Black Power* is focused on the impact of the first black president of the United States and its significance in the context of black freedom struggle, in every conversation, we also took time to explore the profound importance and meaning of the fact that the First Family is a black family, and how it projects a glowing example of black love, dignity, and family values.

"When Michelle Obama got to be the cover girl on *Vogue*, every brown girl who was told she was too brown, too tall, butt too big, too this, too that, got to be a cover girl in that moment," says WBAI host and producer of the *Emotional Justice* series, Esther Armah. "The history of those images, in the future, may be more powerful than whatever policy was or was not mastered in the time that Barack Obama was in the White House."

Dr. Vincent Harding, veteran civil rights activist and colleague of Martin Luther King, says that understanding the historic power and possibilities that the First Family and President Obama present to black Americans involves understanding the full trajectory of black history in the United States as a "movement for the expansion and deepening of democracy in America."

Hundreds of years of enslavement, abuse, and denial of rights by white society set the course for race relations in the United States. When the first Africans arrived in Jamestown, Virginia, in 1619, the white people who enslaved them did not consider them to be human; they were commodities, livestock, meant to be bought, sold, bred, and used for work. Over the lifetime of the trans-Atlantic slave trade, twelve million Africans would be herded across the ocean in cramped boats like cattle.[7] These people were beaten, abused, and traded; women raped and their children consigned to lives of oppression, forced labor, and misery. Adding to the horror is the fact that the U.S. legal system long enforced the right of whites to enslave people of color; in fact, one in four U.S. presidents were directly involved in human trafficking.[8]

Black history has been shaped and defined by resistance to the reality of these facts and the relentless, multigenerational effort to abolish the injustices perpetuated over the ages. Early efforts to redress the issue include the signing of the Emancipation Proclamation and the adoption of the Thirteenth and Fourteenth Amendments in the 1860s to the attempts to "recognize the equality of all men before the law" via the Civil Rights Act of 1875 during the Reconstruction Era.

Jim Crow laws establishing "separate by equal" would strangle attempts for equality for almost one hundred years until the landmark United States Supreme Court case *Brown v. Board of Education* in 1954 which ended segregation, at least on paper. Out of this grew the broad black freedom movement of which struggles for civil rights and black power were part. Only sixty years ago, much of the country enforced a state of racial apartheid. Blacks, people of color, and progressives organized, marched, and confronted the white-dominated system. They fought for dignity, equal rights, voting rights, and fairness for all across the full spectrum of life—housing, education, health, employment, and cultural expression. Their voices, vision and victories gave birth to yet new struggles.

Progress, of course, has been made and greater freedoms

are enjoyed today. But there are almost constant reminders that entrenched racial injustice persists at many levels. In addition to well-known flashpoints like the 1992 Los Angeles Riots, the 1999 shooting of Guinean immigrant Amadou Diallo in New York City, the Jena Six case, and the execution-style killing of Oscar Grant in Oakland, California, in 2009, people of color in the United States continue to suffer greater rates of incarceration, unemployment, housing discrimination, and significantly lower levels of wealth than do whites. A study published by the Pew Institute in July 2011 revealed, "Median wealth of whites is now 20 times that of black households and 18 times that of Hispanic households, double the already marked disparities that had prevailed in the decades before the recent recession."[9] "We have not ended racial caste in America," writes Michelle Alexander, "we have merely redesigned it."[10]

Further studies focusing on education, child poverty, and home foreclosure offer little respite from the gloomy forecast for black America. A 2010 report from the Schott Foundation revealed just 47 percent of African American males graduated from high school in the 2007/8 academic year.[11] The poverty rate for black children is 36 percent, compared to 12 percent for non-Hispanic whites[12]; and on the housing front, African American and Latino homeowners are expected to lose an estimated 350 billion dollars in wealth due to the ongoing foreclosure crisis.[13] It's clear that more needs to be done to address the "unfinished task of emancipation."[14] How, if at all, will the first African American presidency help the United States to better address that task and the many challenges outlined through our roundtable discussions and the conversations presented in this book?

Historians, community organizers, activists, and others will likely continue to ask that question for years to come. It is, however, a point of discussion today, and it is this national and global conversation of which the Redefining Black Power project is a part.

Just as the voices in the Pacifica Radio Archives provide an audio connection to the hearts, minds, and voices of the black freedom movement over fifty years ago, it is our vision that this project will begin to build connections around the issues being faced today with an awareness of the possibilities, history, concerns, and expectations of a cross section of progressive black intellectuals and community activists.

This book is not, and never set out to be, a work of academic rigor or an anthology of the key players in the black freedom movement. Instead, this book, coupled with the roundtable discussions and audio documentaries produced and aired on the Pacifica Radio Network, provides a marker in history, a snapshot in time, and a starting point for ongoing conversations about the past, present, and future of black America.

As a voice for social change, the final chapter and the third phase of the Redefining Black Power project belongs to you. Technology and social media changed the dynamic of the 2008 election, and this project, too, is embracing the Internet's power as a tool for organizing, movement building, and contributing to the unfinished task of emancipation.

We invite you, the reader, to participate in the conversation. Lay down your marker in history by sharing your stories, thoughts, and opinions at www.redefiningblackpower .com or join us on Facebook or Twitter.

All of the conversations held support a common vision:

we have come a long way, we've had great victories, but we are far from living in a post-racial society. Social change comes from the people, from the bottom up, from the community out. If the Obama White House uplifts our communities, ultimately it will be because the people organized, spoke out, and pushed for the changes that are so urgently needed. Historic opportunity exists side by side with economic, political, cultural injustice, a crisis of unemployment, and ongoing violence against and within the black community. As Jay-Z and Kanye West rap on their album, *Watch the Throne*:

> And I'm from the murder capital, where they murder
>   for capital
> Heard about at least 3 killings this afternoon
> Lookin' at the news like damn I was just with him after
>   school,
> No shop class but half the school got a tool,
> And I could die any day type attitude
> Plus his little brother got shot reppin' his avenue
> It's time for us to stop and re-define black power

Joanne Griffith

24

ONE

The Movement for the Expansion and Deepening of Democracy in America

A Conversation of Context with Dr. Vincent Harding

What is the definition of civil rights? According to the *Merriam-Webster* dictionary, civil rights are "the nonpolitical rights of a citizen; *especially*: the rights of personal liberty guaranteed to United States citizens by the 13th and 14th amendments to the Constitution and by acts of Congress."

This definition provides a legal foundation upon which rights can be built. Just look at the Thirteenth and Fourteenth Amendments. The former abolished slavery; the latter established citizenship rights and due process of law to all those born on U.S. soil. But can simplistic explanations of civil rights ever fully define the profound interpersonal intricacies of a movement?

Just like any good student, I spent many weeks rereading well-thumbed civil rights reference books in my collection, going over newspaper articles, speaking with scholars and listening to audio archives as I approached guests for interview. The schedule set, I arrived in Denver, Colorado, for my first conversation armed with questions, reference points, a recorder, and notepad. I was ready to absorb the life lessons of Dr. Vincent Harding.

I was a fan of Dr. Harding's work long before the journey of this book began. I didn't know him personally, but felt I knew the concerns of his heart from the words he wrote as a speechwriter for Dr. Martin Luther King Jr. In preparing for my time with Dr. Harding, I listened to some of the oratory works he penned for Dr. King, including the famous antiwar speech, "A Time to Break Silence," which King delivered on April 4, 1967, at Riverside Church in New York City.

Unlike many of King's speeches before it, "A Time to Break Silence" stands out for confronting the inconsistencies of U.S. foreign policy and militarism. Dr. King's voice is both weary and urgent as he outlines his opposition to the U.S. war in Vietnam and the need to defeat "the giant triplets of racism, extreme materialism, and militarism."[15] This issue clearly weighed heavily on Dr. King's heart, a burden shared by Dr. Vincent Harding, the man who scribed those words and felt the pain of every one. Dr. Harding was Dr. King's friend, confidante, and brother at arms.

I first made contact with Dr. Vincent Harding while working on a show for the BBC to mark the fortieth anniversary of Dr. King's assassination. It was only then I realized I was speaking with the man who wrote those powerful words unleashed by Dr. King at Riverside Church that so moved me and opened my eyes to another dimension of this icon of the civil rights era.

Although not the first name to be mentioned in conversations about the black freedom movements, Dr. Harding has been an ever present force in the struggle since the 1950s and a significant voice and contributor in the fight for African American agency. As representatives of the Mennonite Church, Harding and his wife, fellow activist Rosemarie Freeney Harding, moved to Atlanta, Georgia, in 1960 and founded Mennonite House, a refuge for activists and fellow supporters of nonviolent protest. Their work stretched beyond Mennonite House to supporting antisegregation campaigns with the Student Nonviolent Coordinating Committee, the Congress of Racial Equality, and the Southern Christian Leadership.

A man of many dimensions, Dr. Harding was the first director of the Martin Luther King Jr. Memorial Center and taught at Spelman College, Temple University, and the University of Pennsylvania. Continuing a lifetime of service, the theologian, historian, and activist is currently chairperson of the Veterans of Hope Project, an educational initiative on religion, culture, and participatory democracy based at Iliff School of Theology in Denver, Colorado. Titles mean little to Dr. Harding, but the importance of accuracy as it pertains to the civil rights movement and its goals are of paramount importance to him, including what the term "civil rights movement" really means.

We met in his office at Iliff. The room was lined on almost all sides with books; Dr. Harding's own works, materials for research purposes, and other papers. Ever the educator, he gave me homework before we met: to read a paper he wrote in 1968 entitled "The Religion of Black Power." It examines the intersection of faith and the black power movement, the rejection and deep-seated mistrust of Christianity, and the installation of faith-based principles to achieve equality. As Harding states in the piece:

In spite of the tendency of Black Power advocates to repress any reference to the earlier Afro-American religious expressions—especially as they were found in the non-violent movement—the most familiar word of the past remains available to set the stage for an exploration of the religious exploration of the current themes. At a forum on Black Power in Atlanta during the fall of 1966, while discussing love, a spokesman for Black Power was heard to say "Martin Luther King was trying to get us to love white folks before we learned to love ourselves, and that ain't no good."[16]

Our original plan was to discuss religion, black power, and the civil rights movement. We did, but our conversation went further. With careful consideration and a slow, deliberate exhalation of words, Dr. Harding laid the foundation of *Redefining Black Power*.

Vincent: "The civil rights movement" is a convenient journalistic term, but the longer I live, the more I am certain that "the civil rights movement" is an absolutely inadequate way of talking about this great, transformative movement that many of us were deeply involved in and that many of us continue to be deeply involved in. I prefer "the movement for the expansion and deepening of democracy in America." And so, whenever you say "civil rights movement," I'm going to be hearing "the movement for the expansion and deepening of democracy in America," that was manifested, at one point, in something we called "the civil rights movement."

Joanne: Give us an explanation as to what that means, "the movement for the expansion and deepening of democracy in America"?

Vincent: There's a wonderful book by a woman named Constance Curry, called *Silver Rights*, in which she is talking particularly about some of the magnificent grassroots people from the black community who worked to transform Mississippi, specifically. They did not find any meaning in the term "civil rights" to describe what they were about. Again and again, they referred to "silver rights" which had meaning for them, because "silver" was something that had value. Constance Curry uses it as an epigram to her book, words from an essay by Alice Walker. Alice shares with me the same conviction that "civil rights" is essentially a legalistic term. The work for gaining certain legal rights is important, but not a definitional way of describing the long journey that many of us have been on and that had a particular set of high points in the 1950s and 1960s. It was always about more than the gaining of rights.

Joanne: What was it about, if it was about more than the gaining of rights?

Vincent: One of the most important things that became clear, was a term that very many people often used when I first met them, especially in the local communities of the South in the 1950s and 1960s. They talked about working to gain and maintain their *dignity*. For them, the movement was about proclaiming the fullness of their humanity, which was being denied by all of the processes of white domination, segregation, and violence. All of those things, consciously and unconsciously, were meant to diminish the black person's appreciation for their own beauty, for their own significance, for their own power, for their own possibilities. So, for many people, one of the great goals of the movement was to regain their sense of what we would now call "agency." They did not use that term then, always the term "dignity" instead.

On the larger level, it was a struggle to place real meaning in the words of democracy. Dr. King spoke to this point on December 5, 1955, just days after Rosa Parks was arrested for refusing to give up her seat to a white passenger. He delivered a speech at the first official gathering of the Montgomery Improvement Association at Holt Street Baptist Church. There he said:

> We are here this evening for serious business. We are here in a general sense because first and foremost we are American citizens . . . and we are determined to apply our citizenship to the fullness of its meaning. We are here also because of our love for democracy, because of our deep-seated belief that democracy transformed from thin paper to thick action is the greatest form of government on earth.[17]

So, all of this is, essentially, to focus attention on the fact that any legal description of what our movement was about, is inadequate, off-putting and, on some levels, dangerous.

If we were to take "the civil rights movement" to simply be the accomplishment of legal actions then we would have an incomplete and flawed concept. For example, if numerous legal actions and Constitutional laws needed to get passed, then, once that is done, one might think that the work of the "civil rights movement" was complete.

Once you have people able to sit where they couldn't sit, to go to school where they couldn't go to school, to be in offices of political power when they couldn't, if your definition is simply "legal rights," then for a younger generation, when they see the many laws, the many new people, the many new faces, the many new places, they could easily think, "Well, that work has been done. Let me now go on to earn as much money as I can for my life's vocation."

But, if we can see this as a part of an ongoing task of the work to create *a more perfect union*, the work to follow-up on the Preamble to the Constitution about our country, then we can see that we're talking about what happened when, for a particular period of time, some very powerful and beautiful people took on the task of changing laws and changing status as a part of the larger work of expanding democracy to the people who were historically denied it by racial laws.

If, however, we can see that work of creating new laws not as an end it itself but as a part of the ongoing struggle of the *deepening of the meaning of democracy*, then it becomes our job in every proceeding generation to do the work again and again and again. That's what I mean by the expansion of democracy, the deepening of the meaning of democracy and, obviously, at this point in history, to try to understand what a multiracial, multireligious society based on the democratic possibilities of its entire people can possibly mean.

The civil rights movement was an important part of that long history. Now, the history continues and "civil rights," as we call them, are not the focus anymore. Some people have, understandably, transferred the terminology into "human rights," but I am still convinced that the great power that I saw in the magnificent women and men and children who were working in the movement, that that power cannot be confined to a fight for rights. We were fighting for our humanity. We were fighting for the fullest expression of our human possibilities and we had, whether we used terminology or not, a vision of the best possibilities of this country that it was not, in any way, achieving. In the terms that James Baldwin so often used, we were trying to understand what it meant for us to "achieve" ourselves. And so, that long, long, long rumination is part of what I feel is necessary for me to define what I mean when I hear the term "civil rights movement."

Joanne: Would you use a similar definition, or something different, to define "black power"?

Vincent: The black power movement was also focusing on the matter of human dignity. It was a new way that black people began to exert power to define ourselves. It was a way of seizing the responsibility to speak our own words, in our own way, about who we are. That's one thing that it meant to me.

It was also, for some people, a very narrowly defined idea of simply the black side of white power. "If you guys have power to mess us up, we're gonna have power and, if we can, we're going to mess you up!" For me, that is a reflexive response to a negative experience; by getting involved in more negativity ourselves. On the other hand, I saw in the heart of black power a call for black people to learn how to love ourselves and, for me, that was one of its most powerful meanings; the attempt not only to define ourselves and speak for ourselves, but to value ourselves and to love ourselves on our terms.

In spite of our uncomfortableness with the word *love*, for me, wherever people are trying to love, I want to be there and I want to encourage it. That is an important part of what black power meant for me.

Joanne: Why was there discomfort with the word *love* in the black power movement?

Vincent: Because it was associated with what they understood to be King's, and nonviolent practitioners' concept of love. Without understanding the powerful strength of love, they were seeing love as an expression of weakness and not one of strength. They did not want to be involved in any way in the human vulnerability that comes wherever real love is. Even though they didn't like it, very often they were using it in connection to how black people needed to relate to each other, to love each other.

Joanne: You talk about the differences in how the concept of "love" was perceived by those within the civil rights and black power movements, but there were also differences in the way in which each group fought for rights. How did other differences manifest between the two "camps"?

Vincent: Part of the "two camp" description was a journalistic short-circuiting of the fullness of ideas and the fullness of experience. It was a journalistic attempt to set up an easy way to describe a situation. But, part of it had to do with something that was really deep.

Many of the people who were close to the kind of ideas and practices that King represented, and I would include myself among that group, understood the work that they were doing as "fighting." It was not "not fighting." It *was* fighting, but it was fighting using weapons that were not those of the oppressor that could only be oppressive in their character. To seek for the best possibilities of *the other* was one of the deepest and integral understandings of what nonviolence was about. The struggle was then not to destroy the other, but to actually *help* the other discover their own best possibilities by refusing to accept their definition of reality; by refusing to do what they said was lawful or legal. By refusing to return their hate with other hate; by refusing to let them set the agenda for how the fight should go on—this was one of the most important differences between two ways of engaging in the struggle for freedom.

Joanne: Within your paper "Religion and Black Power," published in 1968, you talk about this at length. Why do you think that some within the black power movement were against a more faith or spiritually based approach to dealing with the oppressor?

Vincent: Part of it was the understandable mistrust that so many people had of religion. Religion has so often been used to manipulate the weak, the poor, the oppressed. Historically it had been used to push people to accept their situation rather than organize and fight to improve it. People in the movement who stood against what they understood to be religious approaches were afraid of those uses of religion.

They were not recognizing that religion was a double-edged sword, one that could destroy people by its misuse, but that could also transform people into new possibilities by its best use. I think a lot of folks did not want to deal with all that subtlety. They wanted to cut to the quick, cut to the chase. They were, in other words, very American, in spite of the fact that they were so down on America. That, for me, was one of the great ironies. That they were ready to pick up the American love of the gun, pick up the American belief in solving things through violence. They were willing to pick up the American impatience with anything that took time. And so, that was all a part of it, that they themselves were much more American than they thought.

Joanne: They were utilizing their constitutional right to bear arms. . . .

Vincent: Without a doubt, without a doubt.

Joanne: In the same paper, "The Religion of Black Power," from 1968, you do discuss a number of ways in which the black power movement in itself was almost a kind of religion.

Vincent: Well, I think, what I was trying to say really is that, in spite of, or because of, their flight from traditional religion, they developed some very important practices and ideas that could be called "religious" and could be connected to some of the best aspects of religion all over the world.

For one thing, their emphasis was on how to work with the weakest, most outcast, and most beaten up people. And that was one of the most important contributions that the black power movement made to the black community. There was, and still is, a strand of thought in the black community that, like our dear President Obama, is very middle-class oriented. Even back then one of the most important teachings of many of the black power practitioners was their insistence that we stand with the poor, that we identify with the poor and, of course, King, himself, very clearly saw that. That is why I don't accept the "two camps" thing, because that is what he said very explicitly. "I choose to identify with the poor." King made that very clear, not just in his words, but by the fact that he chose to give his life to a struggle of garbage workers.

So that focus of the black power folks on the weakest, the most disadvantaged, and the most abused was a very religious direction that is called for by the best religious thinking and actions of the real community. So even those who claim consciously to reject religion, they don't really reject the truth that goes under religion and that comes up to us through religion. They reject the stuff that they've seen built around religion that has not been good and, in many cases, has been toxic for the best human development.

Joanne: Your life has been dedicated to the complex and ongoing fight for the deepening of democracy in the United States. Why did you and your wife, Rosemarie, feel compelled to be involved in the struggle of black America?

Vincent: Rosemarie and I met each other in Chicago. She was part of a family of twelve siblings and they had come to Chicago, like so many millions, from the South, particularly out of southwest Georgia. I had grown up in New York, in Harlem and the South Bronx, and I had been drafted into the army.

It was while I was in basic training, learning how to be an

effective killer, I began asking myself what did that training have to do with the religious community that I had grown up in, where they placed great, great emphasis on obeying the teachings of the Bible. When I left that community to go into the military, I found myself reading the Bible for the first time. It was in the context of that personal engagement with the Jesus of the Bible and with his teachings about the way you deal with enemies, that by the time I left the military, I was clearly a conscientious objector to war as a way of dealing with enemies.

By the time I got to the University of Chicago, I discovered that there was a whole Christian tradition about which I knew nothing—the so-called "peace churches" of the Quakers and Brethren and Mennonites, who actually taught nonviolence and, in many cases, had lived very valiant lives opposing the ways of war. Some of them had given their lives in opposition to being conscripted into military forces and I came in touch, for the first time, with one of those groups myself, the Mennonite Church. In the course of that, I met Rosemarie, who had already been a part of that Mennonite Church community and who shared much of the same convictions about the teachings of Jesus and how seriously they were meant to be taken.

I first met Martin Luther King back in 1958 and had a wonderful initial contact. He reminded me that Mennonites knew something about nonviolence and the teachings of Jesus on how to deal with enemies and that that's what he was trying to do in the South. He said, essentially, "You ought to come down here and help us out."

Rose and I, still based in Chicago at the time, kept saying to the Mennonites, "We ought to be there." Eventually, the

leaders of the various service organizations of the predomi-
nantly white Mennonite Church began to say, "Well, our
church should be present on that battleground." But, as so
often happens to people who raise those kinds of questions,
they looked at us and said, "And you go on our behalf."

Joanne: As representatives.

Vincent: Exactly. That was exactly the term. Rose and I then
were asked to go South as Mennonite representatives to the
freedom movement. That was our self-developed description
and we went because we belonged. We believed that that was
an important struggle; that experimenting with the way of
nonviolent resistance to the powers of segregation and experimenting with the ways of nonviolent resistance to white
terrorism was worth exploring and participating in.

We moved to Atlanta and began to develop an institution called Mennonite House. It became a kind of movement
safe house for people to come and rest and find relief and talk
and discuss and debate and think about what we were doing.
From that base, we travelled all through the South, sometimes at the request of King or SNCC, the Student Nonviolent Coordinating Committee, or other movement folks, to
encourage people and let them know that there were others
who were on their side.

We were also sometimes asked to teach the ways of nonviolence. One of the most interesting things that we were
called upon to do was to try to make contact with white people in the South who had some kind of conscience. Some
white people—and white Christians especially—were trying
to figure out what they should do in the midst of trying to

wrestle with their own faith, about what their faith meant for them to be and to do something other than simply sticking with the white line.

Joanne: Because I guess the teachings are still the same for everyone, "Love thy neighbour as yourself."

Vincent: "Love thy neighbor as yourself." About that there was no question. But for whites, the South was full of black neighbors and black fellow Christians and the question then had to become, "What do you do about this?" Part of our work was to encourage them not to run away from those questions, but to try to find some ways to take them on and to act on them.

Joanne: One of the often-raised debates relating to the fight for African American rights is that of integration or separation; those who said "We have to try to integrate, as a people, with white society," as opposed to "We should reject white society and build our own community." What are your thoughts on this?

Vincent: You're touching on one of the most important of the continuing discussions, explorations, debates that we have to pick up because, unless we pick this up and wrestle with it, we will be in great trouble.

There are always more than those two alternatives; to either *assimilate*—which is what people very often meant by integrate—or *stand away*, condemn and maybe at the most extreme level, hate. There was always another set of ways of thinking about this that, in some ways, continues on.

As free human beings who are discovering our deepest levels of identity, do we black people really want to make entering the American mainstream our ultimate goal? Or do we see, as a result of reviewing ourselves, the possibility that a new river is needed in America and that our job is not to jump into the old one called "the mainstream," but to help create a new river that will provide a very different set of experiences for our children and everybody's children?

After desegregation, the breaking down of the laws of separation, what does integration mean? It is clear that, by-and-large, we don't know. We are still, essentially, living separated lives, particularly in our residential patterns, due to economic and racial factors.

Our children—especially the children of the working class and poorer classes—are still going to what are, essentially, segregated schools, or at least separated schools. And we still need to ask what would an integrated school system look like, be like? What would an integrated religious community look like? What would an integrated law practice look like? What would an integrated journalism practice look like? I think that we still have a long way to go on these matters. That is part of what I am mean by the term "the deepening of democracy."

Joanne: Do you think democracy was deepened by the election of Barack Obama?

Vincent: The election provided, and provides, a greater opportunity for the deepening of democracy than we've had up to now, but it in itself was not necessarily a deepening. On many levels, *the campaign* was an example of a deeper democracy.

Joanne: Why was the campaign an example of a deepening of democracy, but not the actual election of Barack Obama himself?

Vincent: The campaign engaged all kinds of people who had been outside, or on the edges of society. Just numerically, there were more people who had never been engaged in democratic community-building. There were more people who never thought of themselves in terms of the potential created by their participation. In some cases, it was just the simple act of voting. I met many people in the North, and I think particularly of black people now, who had never voted before and who did not feel that they had ever had anything to vote for before. So I think the campaign was a part of the story—the bringing in of multiracial groups of younger people. Those were all part of what I mean by the "campaign," as opposed to the administration.

Joanne: Did you ever think that you would see a black president in your lifetime?

Vincent: The issue of a black president was never an active concern of my mind. The issue of black people participating in the transformation of American society, as people, is where I have always been, remembering, especially, all of the magnificent black young people, black old people who I ran into in the South. For me, that has always been the focus of my thinking about "Could this happen in America?" Outside of Mississippi and Alabama and Georgia, how could we gain that kind of deep participation of all kinds of black people? A black president was never an issue for me.

The important thing is that, at his best, Obama can inspire black people and other people of color to recognize that, ultimately, it is *We, the People of the United States* who are called upon to do the deepest work. As I wrote to him through a friend during the campaign, I asked him to stop trying to convince people about what a wonderful commander-in-chief he would be, but to go back to his own roots and think about what it might mean to be "community organizer-in-chief," that we need that more than we need commanders-in-chief.

Joanne: Did you get a response?

Vincent: Oh, no. I didn't expect to, but that was all right.

Joanne: Speaking of President Obama, in the past you have written about "black Messiahs"—Marcus Garvey, Dr. Martin Luther King Jr., Malcolm X, and others. Is there a danger that people have grabbed onto President Obama and expect such great things from him, that he's being set up to fail?

Vincent: Consider the possibility, Joanne, that the greatest danger is not our setting *him* up to fail, but our setting *ourselves* up to fail, and we fail once we place all of that focus on him; that's failure of a democratic society itself. So, yes, I think that we set up the situation for democratic failure when we see him as the answer to the problems of the nation and he fails if he doesn't mobilize us—not just to keep him in office, but to recognize what it is the nation needs to become a more humane and creative society.

Joanne: Has this been a problem for some of America's other black leaders, for example Marcus Garvey, or Dr. King, with whom you worked with closely? Do we place too much at their door?

Vincent: Well, part of the difficulty was that, in some cases, they helped to create a difficulty. In some ways, they helped create it because a lot of ego stuff can develop when people start worshipping you. But in some ways, they helped to create it out of the best intentions; that is, feeling "I must do this." That's a very tricky line, between a sense of deep responsibility for living the life that I've been given, on the one hand, or a sense that "I am the only one who can do this and therefore I must do it" on the other. Once you get into that kind of thinking, there will be lots of people who will encourage you along that way, again, partly for good reasons, but sometimes simply because if you encourage "her" to do it, then that means you don't have to do it. There is always something in us that is fighting towards that tendency, to build the Messiah so that we do not do any saving work ourselves.

TWO

What about the Brother at the Bottom of the Well?

Law in the Age of Obama with Professor Michelle Alexander

In 1903, prolific author, activist, and educator W. E. B. DuBois outlined the relationship between African Americans and the U.S. legal system in his seminal work, *The Souls of Black Folk*:

> Daily the Negro is coming more and more to look upon law and justice, not as protecting safeguards, but as sources of humiliation and oppression. The laws are made by men who have little interest in him; they are executed by men who have absolutely no motive for treating the black people with courtesy or consideration; and, finally, the accused law-breaker is tried, not by his peers, but too often by men who would rather punish ten innocent Negroes than let one guilty one escape.[18]

So what has changed in the almost ninety years since DuBois penned these words? Some may answer, "not much." Recalling painful memories of police brutality in the

United States doesn't take long: the 1991 beating of Rodney King in Los Angeles, the fatal shooting of Oscar Grant in the opening hours of 2009 on the floor of an Oakland, California, transit station, and the gunning down of innocent citizens in search of help in the aftermath of Hurricane Katrina on the Danziger Bridge in New Orleans in 2005.

Brutality also comes in the guise of racial profiling and controversial stop-and-frisk practices. Deemed constitutional by the 1968 U.S. Supreme Court ruling *Terry v. Ohio*, police officers can stop any pedestrian or motorist they have a "reasonable suspicion" of partaking in nefarious behaviour. Statistically, many of those people are black. Figures released by the American Civil Liberties Union show that in 2009, 70 percent of people stopped in Philadelphia were African American. Just 8.5 percent of the total stops made that year resulted in an arrest. In New York City, that figure was 53 percent. African Americans make up 26 percent of the city's population. Yet pleas against racial profiling are met with reassurances from officials that stop and frisk is about crime, not race. The numbers tell another story, and we have yet to get to the disproportionate number of African Americans behind bars.

Just like the words of DuBois, black nationalist Marcus Garvey's twentieth-century musings reflect today's reality for many African Americans, men especially:

That we suffer so much today under whatsoever
flag we live is proof positive that constitutions and
laws, when framed by the early advocates of human
liberty, never included and were never intended
for us as a people. It is only a question of sheer

accident that we happen to be fellow citizens today with the descendants of those who, through their advocacy, laid the foundation for human rights.[19]

The apparent unfairness of the U.S. legal system is an open wound that has provoked professors, social commentators, and ordinary folks to question just who is protected by the "rights" set out by the Founding Fathers in the United States's supreme legal document, the Constitution and its amendments.

As I went through the piles of contacts of legal scholars who could speak on the impact of the law on black America, I opened a message about a new book entitled *The New Jim Crow: Mass Incarceration in the Age of Colorblindness.* The Jim Crow laws enacted between 1876 and 1965 mandated "separate, but equal," resulting in segregation and a widespread abuse of African Americans. The "new" Jim Crow puts black people in jail and throws away the key.

In her book, Michelle Alexander, a civil rights advocate, litigator, and legal scholar, uses the power of education, research, personal experience, and the written word to shine a light on a problem that pervades the criminal justice system, with little resolution in sight.

On sabbatical from her post at Ohio State University, Michelle and I met in Los Angeles during her book tour. Her vibrant energy and enormous commitment to right so many wrongs filled an empty music studio at Pacifica station, KPFK.

Michelle: Even when I cast my vote for Barack Obama, I didn't fully believe he could win. When he did, I was at an election-night party in support of Obama in downtown

Columbus, Ohio, and I was stunned. I was elated—almost flabbergasted—that it had actually happened. I remember looking around, seeing people hugging and crying with tears streaming down their faces. It was surreal.

As we poured out of the building, full of joy and hope, I saw a black man, handcuffed behind his back and on his knees in the gutter. There were four or five police officers around him in a semicircle, just laughing, joking, shooting the breeze; utterly oblivious to this man's human existence. All of the folks streaming out of the party glanced over at him, then averted their gaze and carried on. I just remember thinking, "What does the election of Barack Obama mean for him? This man in the gutter?"

Now that much of the euphoria of Obama's win has worn off, I think that question speaks louder than before. For poor folks of color, it's unclear if the election of Barack Obama really means anything for them. We need to hold Obama and our black and brown leadership accountable for the ways in which they've been blind to the folks at the bottom of the well, to use Derrick Bell's words.

We have to hold ourselves accountable, too. Those of us in the civil rights community who have not made the folks at the bottom of the well our top priority, and all of us who have turned away from the man on his knees in the gutter. We all share a responsibility for where we are today. How, in the so-called "Age of Obama," can there be more African American men under correctional control, in prison or jail, on probation or parole, than were enslaved in 1850? We all share some measure of responsibility, not only for the racial reality of today, but also for its solution.

Joanne: Why do you think that, be it civil rights activist, lawyer, or ordinary man or woman on the street, we are not paying attention to those people at the bottom of the well? What's going on there?

Michelle: There are a number of things going on. First, civil rights organizations. If you take a look at the history of racial justice advocacy, you can see that a primary method or strategy for racial justice advocates has been to try to identify people who seem to have greater moral virtue and lift them up as examples; people who defy racial stereotypes.

Joanne: A good example of this is Claudette Colvin. Back in March 1955, she refused to give up her seat on a bus in Montgomery, nine months before Rosa Parks did the same thing. The difference being that she was fifteen, pregnant, and unmarried, so not deemed an upstanding citizen in that way. Racial justice advocates passed her over as an example.

Michelle: Exactly. Claudette was viewed as not having good character. They wanted to find someone who defied racial stereotypes, who white people might respect. Then another woman, Mary Louise Smith, was rejected not because of anything she had done, but because her father was rumored, falsely, to be an alcoholic. Even that negative association was enough for them to disqualify her as a potential plaintiff.

Civil rights advocates, for a long, long time, have deliberately tried to shield from public view those aspects of the African American community that seem to confirm racial stereotypes or reflect the "worst aspects" of our community. However, in challenging racial bias in the criminal justice system, or seeking to dismantle the system of mass incarceration, that strategy doesn't work so well. In this current era, so many people have been branded and labeled as criminals. If we, as civil rights advocates, aren't willing to embrace those who have been branded or embrace the people at the bottom of the well, then there is little hope that we are ever going to dismantle the system of mass incarceration, or bring an end to bias in the criminal justice system.

Joanne: In the dictionary, a civil right is defined as "an enforceable right or privilege that, if interfered with by another, gives rise to an action for inquiry. Examples of civil rights are freedom of speech, press and assembly, the right to vote, freedom from involuntary servitude and the right to equality in public places." The definition is more detailed and continues, but what is your definition of "civil rights" in this "Age of Obama"?

Michelle: One of the things that we have learned, and that both Dr. Martin Luther King Jr. and Malcolm X shared at the end of their lives, is that "civil rights" don't buy you much. Civil rights are relatively limited; that what we need is a transition from the era of fighting for civil rights to an era of fighting for human rights. Human rights are ultimately those rights that transcend race, class, and prior criminal history. Human rights can never be forfeited and they're basic to all human beings, whether you're viewed as guilty or innocent, citizen or immigrant. Human rights ensure that everyone, no matter who they are or what they've done or where they're from, has the right to work, has the right to food, has the right to shelter, has the right to security. Without these basic human rights, the right to vote doesn't buy you very much.

As a result, what we've seen in our democracy is that the power of money is greater than the power of the vote. Without any recognition of basic human rights, people who are poor or people who are marginalized can find themselves without work, without food, without basic shelter. Today, once you've been branded a felon, you no longer have the right to be treated fairly in the employment process. Employment discrimination is perfectly legal. Housing discrimination is perfectly legal. In fact, once you're branded a felon, you're barred by law for a minimum of five years from public housing. Where are these folks supposed to go? If you're branded a "drug felon," you're denied food stamps for the rest of your life.

Joanne: From colonial days to now, certain pieces of legislation have been enacted to include African Americans in the democratic process. Just take us through some of the key legislative benchmarks in the fight for civil rights, but also some of the legal barriers that have excluded people from their civil and human rights.

Michelle: Obviously the 13th Amendment, to abolish slavery. That's a big one.

Joanne: Let's start there.

Michelle: What's fascinating is that the Thirteenth Amendment has an exception in it. It abolishes slavery, except for forced labor in prison. Here you have the Thirteenth Amendment essentially foreshadowing the emergence of a future caste system. Then, you have the Fifteenth Amendment, prohibiting discrimination in voting on the basis of race. But the Fifteenth Amendment also has an exception, for felons. Felons may be denied the right to vote according to the Fifteenth Amendment. The Constitution created loopholes for those who have been labeled criminals.

Moving on from the Thirteenth and Fifteenth Amendments, many people view *Brown v. Board of Education* as the next great landmark in civil rights history.

Joanne: In 1954. This ended segregation in schools, or, some may argue, allegedly ended segregation in schools in the South.

Michelle: Allegedly, yes. In history books, *Brown v. Board of Education* is celebrated as this great triumph over Jim Crow segregation, but the reality is that *Brown v. Board of Education* changed almost nothing in the South. A full decade after *Brown v. Board of Education* was decided, less than 1 percent of Southern schools had desegregated at all. It took a mass movement to bring Jim Crow to its knees. A decision by the high court didn't change anything.

So in terms of legislation that made any real changes, it was the civil rights acts of 1964 and 1965 that marked the end of Jim Crow; or at least the beginning of the end of the old Jim Crow system.

Joanne: In 1965, the impact of Jim Crow laws, nine years shy of their one-hundredth anniversary, was still being felt. Do you think, in some ways, it's actually not a surprise that we're still seeing the residue of Jim Crow today?

Michelle: What's fascinating is how adaptable racism and racial caste systems have proven to be over the years. Since the nation's founding, African Americans have been repeatedly controlled through institutions like slavery and Jim Crow, which appeared to die, but were then reborn in a new form, tailored to the needs and the constraints of the time.

For example, what we saw after the collapse of slavery was plantation owners and the white elite scrambling to figure out how they could continue to exploit black labor. What did they decide to do? They decided to create convict-leasing programs. The police began to round up African American men on extremely minor charges like loitering or vagrancy. They arrested them, sent them to prison, and the prisons then leased them out to plantations in which they were forced to work. The idea was that the prisoners had to earn their freedom. The catch was they could never earn enough to pay back the cost of their clothes and their shelter; they were virtually enslaved again, often for the rest of their lives.

Not long after that, Jim Crow laws emerged as a way of reinstituting a permanent second-class system following the collapse of slavery. Once Jim Crow was defeated by civil rights activists, segregationists began scrambling to develop a new language, since it was no longer socially permissible to say, "Segregation forever!" So, what did they do? They developed the rhetoric and the language of "get tough" and the promise to crack down on crime and welfare mothers. If you trace the history, the same legislators and hard-core segregationists who were a few years earlier shouting, "No black children in my school!" changed their tune to "Oh, it's all about crime. We need to get tough and crack down on them!"

Joanne: What examples can you give of the way the law is used now to control people of color? For example, during an interview on *America's Most Wanted*, President Obama affirmed that the idea of a DNA database was a great idea. What are your thoughts on DNA testing as the latest way to monitor and control people and communities?

Michelle: I think you can put widespread DNA testing of suspected criminals in the same category as gang lists that have been developed in many urban areas around the country. This is where law enforcement officers "sweep" neighborhoods, interviewing everybody on the street, asking for their names, backgrounds, and details on their friends. This information is then entered into a computer database. These same people are then labeled as suspected gang members based on their style of dress, if they have tattoos, or who their friends are. In Denver, there was a gang database that included more than half of the young black men in the city. These kinds of methods of the government trying to achieve near total surveillance over black and brown communities in the name of public safety is really a means of extending and deepening their control over these communities.

This is deeply problematic because youth of color are being labeled either as gang members or drug dealers at a really young age and the cycle begins often before kids are old enough to drive or old enough to vote; they're treated like criminals whether they've done anything or not. Then they're sent to juvenile hall, then prison, and then they're branded felons. They're relegated to a permanent second-class status for life, and the "War on Drugs" has been the primary engine of this new system of control.

Joanne: Just how much of an impact has the "War on Drugs" had?

Michelle: The "War on Drugs" is largely responsible for the *quintupling* of our prison population in just a few short decades. We went from a prison population of about three hundred thousand in the mid-1970s to more than two million, with the greatest increase being driven by drug convictions. Drug convictions account for about two-thirds of the increase in the federal system.

At the state level, more than half of the increase came from drug convictions, and yet study after study shows that people of color are no more likely to use or sell illegal drugs than whites. Yet it's black and brown folks in the hood that have been targeted en masse for precisely the same kind of illegal drug activity that goes on all the time in middle-class and suburban communities, but those kids go off to college.

Joanne: In March 2010, the U.S. Senate reduced the crack cocaine sentencing disparity, what's known as the one-hundred-to-one disparity. Under current law, selling five hundred grams of cocaine subjects defendants to a mandatory five-year prison term, whereas even possessing as little as five grams of crack cocaine subjects defendants to exactly the same penalty. Is the Senate's ruling good news when it comes to dealing with the racial disparity in sentencing when it comes to drugs?

Michelle: Well, here's my problem with this. The Senate has now proposed reducing the one-hundred-to-one disparity to twenty-to-one. Now, this is being heralded as a great advance, but there is still no justification for any disparity at all.

Virtually all of the studies that were offered during the 1980s as a justification for this enormous disparity between crack versus powder cocaine have been discredited. So, why have any disparity at all? To take it one step further, we should be asking, "Why should anyone be put in a cage simply because they possessed some crack cocaine?"

If we were to wish for a loved one to overcome drug addiction or drug abuse, would our recipe be, "Let's put them in a cage and then, when they get out, let's brand them a felon and then subject them to a lifetime of discrimination, scorn, and social exclusion. That'll fix 'em"?

At a basic level, we have to ask ourselves why the United States is essentially alone, among Western democracies, in putting people who use or sell drugs in cages for years or decades of their life. In most European countries, sentences for drug use or sales are measured in days and weeks.

Joanne: If at all. . . .

Michelle: Most people think the drug war is targeted toward rooting out drug kingpins or violent offenders, which is completely false.

Federal funding flows to local and state law enforcement agencies that boost the volume of their drug arrests. If you are wondering why local law enforcement agencies spend so much of their time and energy rounding up people for low-level, nonviolent drug offenses, it's because that's how they get their cash. They don't get rewarded for bringing down drug bosses. In addition, Federal drug forfeiture laws allow state and local law enforcement agencies to keep 80 percent of the cash, cars, and homes that they seize from suspected drug offenders, giving them a direct monetary interest in the profitability of the drug war.

In 2005, four out of five drug arrests were for simple possession. Only one out of five were for sales. Most people in state prison for drug offenses have no history of violence or significant selling activity. So, we're talking about a war that has been waged almost exclusively in poor communities of color, not to root out violent crime or drug kingpins, but to round up as many folks as possible for fairly nonviolent drug offenses. It's a war that's being waged for all the wrong reasons, resulting in a permanent underclass; a lower caste that is defined by law and locked into a second-class status for life.

Joanne: So who benefits from the financial incentives?

Michelle: The Correctional Corporation of America is listed on the New York Stock Exchange. They make big profits warehousing people, human beings. Then, there are all the companies and corporations that serve these prisons; the taser makers, the phone companies that gouge prisoners and their families for the phone calls they make from prison. Long is the list of ways in which American companies profit from the prison industry.

Joanne: In so many ways, what's going on within the legal and criminal justice systems has completely removed elements of power for African Americans. What kind of legal statutes are actually in place to protect those who are branded as felons? Do they have any protection under the law at all?

Michelle: Very little. All of the forms of discrimination I've described that impact felons are perfectly legal. In many states, you can't even get a license to be a barber if you've been branded a felon. It's also not just legal, but required, to deny felons access to public housing. Drug felons are denied food stamps; that denial is legal and required. These forms of discrimination are not just, but they are legal and often *mandated* by law against people.

Then, to the extent one might hope to challenge racial bias in the criminal justice system itself? Good luck! The United States Supreme Court has closed the courthouse doors to claims of racial bias in the criminal justice system at virtually every stage; from stop and search to plea bargaining and sentencing. In a series of cases, including *McCleskey v. Kemp* and *Armstrong v. United States*, the U.S. Supreme Court has specifically said it doesn't matter how severe the racial disparities, it doesn't matter how overwhelming your statistical evidence is; unless you can produce evidence of conscious, intentional racial bias, the kind of evidence that amounts to an admission, you're out of luck.

Joanne: So, how are civil rights advocates tackling this on behalf of people of color who have found themselves behind bars?

Michelle: My own view is that the opportunities for challenging race discrimination in the criminal justice system today are extremely limited; civil rights advocates and racial justice advocates must begin to focus on bottom-up, grassroots organizing and movement building. The sheer scale of the new Jim Crow, this new caste system, is such that, if we wanted to go back to the rates of incarceration that we had in the 1970s, we can't. A time, by the way, when many civil rights activists thought that rates of incarceration were egregiously high.

Joanne: Nothing in comparison to now.

Michelle: If we wanted to just go back to the bad old days of the 1970s, we'd have to release four out of five people who are in prison today—four out of five. More than a million people employed by the criminal justice system could lose their jobs. That's how enormous and entrenched the criminal justice system has become in an exceedingly short period of time.

We could tinker around with the system, but if we're serious about dismantling it, bringing an end to mass incarceration and even returning to the bad old days of the 1970s, then we need to build a movement—a broad-based social movement.

Joanne: And who are the people who are leading this movement now?

Michelle: Well, Barack Obama most certainly is not leading that charge. There are relatively few people who are part of the current black leadership whom we can count on in this regard; but I'm not without hope. There's such inspiring work going on today at the grassroots level. Organizations like All of Us Or None; a group of formerly incarcerated people who have come together to organize for their basic civil and human rights. They're having success with "Ban the Box" campaigns—banning the box on employment applications that authorize discrimination—and helping to inspire others who have been branded to move out of shame and into action.

People like Susan Burton, the founder of A New Way of Life, is also working to support those who have been labeled criminals and providing them a path to safety, security, and social justice activism. It's really my greatest hope that the new leaders that emerge will be those who know best the cruelty of the new caste system and can speak with authenticity about the discrimination that they've faced. So, it may be that our greatest leaders are the ones that we don't yet know by name, but I'm hoping that within a few years that will change.

Joanne: In talking about the black leadership in terms of the legal system, we can look back on the work of Florence Henry, Oliver Hill, and Thurgood Marshall for examples. Who are the activists fighting from the legal corner today? Is it the NAACP? The American Civil Liberties Union?

Michelle: One of my own heroes is Bryan Stevenson. He's the founder of the Equal Justice Initiative in Montgomery, Alabama. He's been fighting for death row inmates, saving many of their lives, and doing legal work that I believe is the greatest model today of civil rights advocacy; blending legal advocacy with community organizing and public education campaigns about the role of racial bias in the system.

There's also Vanita Gupta who helped to lead the legal campaign on behalf of the forty-six people who were rounded up as part of a drug raid in the small town of Tulia, Texas. forty of them were African American, around 15 percent of the town's black population and one-third of Tulia's black men. The raid was based on the word of one unreliable drug informant. They were arrested and incarcerated, and Vanita, a recent law graduate at the time, helped to exonerate them and expose the corruption that existed there. Vanita is now at the ACLU leading the criminal justice program. So, there are people who are doing great work, but my concern is that the civil rights community as a whole has been reluctant to make the War on Drugs and the mass incarceration of people of color a top priority. The tide may be turning. Ben Jealous, executive director of the NAACP, has indicated that he believes that mass incarceration should be among the top priorities of his organization; that's very encouraging.

Joanne: Discussing black leadership leads us back to President Obama and some of the comments that have circulated regarding his views on civil rights. During a speech at Harvard University in 2007, he said: "The teenagers and college students who left their homes to march in the streets of Birmingham and Montgomery, the mothers who walked instead of taking the bus after a long day of doing someone else's laundry and cleaning someone else's kitchen, they didn't brave fire hoses and billy clubs so that their grandchildren and their great-grandchildren would still wonder, at the beginning of the twenty-first century, whether their vote would be counted, whether their civil rights would be protected by their government, whether justice would be equal and opportunity would be theirs. We have more work to do." What do you see as President Obama's steps toward making sure that the work "we need to do" gets done?

Michelle: Right after Barack Obama was elected, he kept reminding us, "Hold me accountable. I can't do this on my own." I think, reading between the lines, he was saying, "Make me do it. Make me do the right thing. I cannot do right, unless you make me." I'm willing to give Barack Obama the benefit of the doubt and believe that he fully intends to honor every campaign pledge he made; that what he said in his inspirational speeches on the campaign trail was not just rhetoric. But the idea that he's just going to get in office and do it himself is not just far-fetched but naive. We should be right under Barack Obama, reminding him over and over again that we put him in office. We did so not just because we wanted to see a black face sitting in the Oval Office, but because we dared to hope that he could actually make a difference in the lives of the folks at the bottom of the well. If he isn't going to do it, we don't need to have him there. That's a tough pill for people to swallow; there really is no point in putting black and brown faces in positions of power if they aren't actually going to make much of a difference. I believe that, to a large extent, affirmative action has masked the severity of racial inequality in the United States. Sprinkling people of color throughout elite institutions gives us the impression that, "Wow, what a long way we've come."

Joanne: Do you think the election of Barack Obama is another distraction, in a way?

Michelle: It's only a distraction if we allow ourselves to be distracted by it; if we fail to convert the energy that was evident in the campaign for Barack Obama, and all the grassroots energy and excitement. If we fail to channel that into real social movements for human rights and for justice, if that doesn't happen, then it will be an empty victory. One of the downsides of affirmative action, and from the existence of a handful of black and brown folks in positions of power, is that it can actually discourage the very kind of mobilization that is necessary for real change to come about. For example, when you have a black police chief, it's often difficult to organize the black community in opposition to police brutality and to racial profiling: to the very kind of tactics of the War on Drugs and mass incarceration which would be interpreted differently if the police chief were white or it was an all-white police force.

We interpret the actions through a different lens once a person of color is implementing the discriminatory policies. We can't allow ourselves to be so easily fooled. It's the policies and the practices that are the issue. Merely changing the complexion of the people in office or those that hold positions of power should not dissuade us or discourage us from doing the hard work that is necessary to change those policies and fight for real social justice.

Joanne: What are your thoughts about the notion that Obama's election brought in a "post-racial" era?

Michelle: Oh, I think the idea that we are in a post-racial period in the United States is just pure fiction. It's this kind of Orwellian doublespeak, and the fact that some people may actually believe what they're saying doesn't make it less tragic.

I think one of the most important things that needs to happen is for us, as a nation, to awake from this color blind slumber that we've been in and awaken to the racial realities of today. As long as we're telling ourselves that we're in a post-racial society, that kind of talk lulls us to sleep and keeps us in a state of complacency and inaction. So before any kind of grand movement can get underway, we've got to wake up to the racial reality of today.

Joanne: In terms of where you see civil rights now, in addition to dealing with this horrendous situation surrounding the large number of African American men who are incarcerated, what are the other civil rights issues that need to be addressed now?

Michelle: Educational inequity. The abysmal state of schools, particularly in urban areas, I think is a terribly neglected issue. Our schools are largely still separate and grossly unequal.

To a large extent, our schools now are really just breeding grounds for prison. Our schools often look like prisons. They feel like prisons. They're really designed, it appears, to prepare kids to go to prison.

Joanne: You mentioned affirmative action earlier. There was a landmark U.S. Supreme Court case in 1978, *Regents of the University of California v. Bakke.* It established that Allan Bakke was discriminated against as a white man due to affirmative action. How has affirmative action played into the way African Americans are treated in the United States today?

Michelle: My thoughts on affirmative action have changed a lot over time. I myself am a beneficiary of affirmative action. I've attended fancy schools in large part because of affirmative action. Many people would say, "You're an affirmative action success story!"

I believe that I was granted a scholarship to Vanderbilt University in part because of my race. It was also because of geography. Vanderbilt, being located in Nashville, Tennessee, was looking to be viewed as less of a regional college or university and more of a national one.

At the time, I was living in Oregon. So recruiting someone from Oregon was part of their geographic affirmative action. But they also, I believe, were interested in recruiting more African Americans. My admission to Stanford Law School, no doubt, was aided by affirmative action.

I can point to numerous instances in my life where an affirmative action policy has been to my personal advantage. But the mere fact that people like me have benefited from affirmative action and gained access to elite institutions does not mean that affirmative action as a policy has had the trickle-down racial justice effect that has been advertised.

I argue in my book that affirmative action has some real downsides that civil rights activists have been extremely reluctant to acknowledge. Affirmative action may have actually helped to mask the emergence of a new racial caste system because affirmative action makes it possible for colored people like me to be sprinkled through elite institutions, while at the same time millions of poor people of color are being rounded up and warehoused in prisons.

Apparent success of people like me, aided by affirmative action, makes it appear as though if only those folks wasting away in our prisons and jails had just tried a little bit harder, they too might have gone to Stanford, or Harvard, or Yale. Affirmative action has created an appearance of fairness in the system that doesn't exist in reality.

Joanne: How then, if we're not using some of the tools that are available to us through government policy or through the legal apparatus in the United States, get beyond the need for initiatives such as affirmative action?

Michelle: The goal isn't to get a few people through the door. The goal is to create equality of opportunity for all, and meaningful access to basic human rights for *all* people.

Unfortunately there aren't structural mechanisms currently in place that will ensure that a poor kid growing up in the hood in Detroit has similar chances to a white kid living in suburbia.

However, that doesn't mean that affirmative action is our panacea instead. I think it suggests that we need to go back to where Dr. Martin Luther King Jr. and the Poor People's Campaign left off and do the hard work of movement building for human rights and for equal and excellent education for people of all colors and from all walks of life; for access to health care and the right to jobs and to economic justice. It's that hard work of movement building that has been avoided for so long by those who prefer affirmative action policies to the hard work of organizing.

Joanne: Let's look at affirmative action this way: if a few make it into an elite institution, what responsibility do people of color who "make it" have to others behind them?

Michelle: Well, there's plenty of evidence that people who do have access to elite institutions do turn around and try to help others. But there's also evidence that there's some mythology about this.

The Harvard professor Lani Guinier offered a persuasive critique of affirmative action in her book *The Miner's Canary*. She points out that traditional strategies for social change—such as those that are rooted in affirmative action and a trickle-down theory of racial justice—are based on this notion that previous outsiders, once given a chance, will exercise power differently.

But the reality is that existing hierarchies and existing institutions discipline newcomers, requiring them to exercise power in the same old ways and play by the same old rules in order to survive. Very often, the newcomers to elite institutions are easily coopted, as they have much to lose and little to gain by challenging the rules of the game.

This dynamic is particularly obvious if you consider the predicament of minority police officers who are charged with waging the drug war. Today, our police organizations look much more like America, far more diverse than they have ever been. Yet those very diverse organizations are waging a brutal and racist drug war against communities populated by people who often look like them. Why is this the case? Well, the structure of our police organizations and the funding that flows through them and all of the ways in which the drug war has been organized and financed, all of those rules and all of that institutional structure guarantee that those who play the role of the police, no matter what their color, are likely to perpetuate forms of racial discrimination whether they harbor any bias, conscious bias, or intent or not.

Police officers of all colors engage in racial profiling. Police officers of all colors engage in stop and frisk operations. Police officers of all colors do that because that's what's expected of them in the drug war and in their organization.

So affirmative action hasn't solved the problem of racial profiling. It hasn't ended the War on Drugs. The reason is that this kind of trickle-down theory of racial justice, if it is not coupled with profound structural reform, just means that the people who are enforcing discriminatory rules now have a different complexion.

Joanne: Would you say that civil rights advocates in the past have placed too much emphasis on affirmative action as a panacea for racial inequality?

Michelle: I do think that too much emphasis has been placed on affirmative action. In fact, judging by the media coverage of affirmative action over the past few decades, one might assume that affirmative action was the main battlefront in race relations today, even as millions of people have been rounded up, placed in cages, branded felons, and then released into a permanent second-class status in the United States through the drug war.

So, yes: I *do* think too much attention has been given to affirmative action and too much faith has been placed in affirmative action to address the racial divide. But, I'm not one of those people who believes affirmative action has done no good. Has affirmative action helped to diversify many of our institutions as well as many of our public agencies? Yes, there's no question about it. But, affirmative action as a strategy for ensuring equal opportunity and closing the racial divide? It's not going to get us there. Affirmative action is not a strategy for addressing the severe and chronic joblessness in inner city communities today; chronic joblessness that has to do with deindustrialization, globalization, and the branding of so many of our young men as felons.

Joanne: How do you continue to see the Obama presidency unfolding, beyond issues of race and equality?

Michelle: My own view is that many of the people who rallied to elect Barack Obama were hoping for much more than they had seen to date. I think there is a significant gap between the promise of his election and the reality, and that many people are disappointed.

No politician in the current political environment is going to be able to deliver the kind of change we hope for. It's our job to change the political environment and build a new public consensus that is rooted in care, compassion, and concern for those who have been locked out, locked up, or marginalized in our society.

Joanne: In light of your thoughts on affirmative action and other race-related issues, how has President Obama's White House changed the conversation surrounding race and racial justice?

Michelle: Obama's election has been used as an excuse by some to argue for the end of affirmative action. There are those that argue that if a black man can be elected president in the United States, then we certainly don't need affirmative action anymore. This reflects people's basic misunderstanding about the extent of racial progress that's been achieved in the United States today and whether the presence of a small number of people at the top is evidence of equal opportunity for all.

However, what has happened with Obama's presidency really should have been predictable. It really isn't that surprising that he has towed to the middle and done his best to avoid the subject of race despite his claim in Philadelphia on the campaign trail that he wanted to inspire a national conversation about race. The fact that he's really tiptoed around it and gone to some great lengths to avoid explicit conversations about race, in retrospect, really shouldn't be surprising.

I think that many of us got caught up with hope and with the enthusiasm and the idealism that was reflected in his campaign. But when push comes to shove, he is a shrewd politician attempting to navigate a difficult political landscape, and he seems to be fairly risk averse.

Joanne: Do you think President Obama does damage by not sufficiently addressing the matter of race?

Michelle: Absolutely. It's a mistake to avoid discussing race. It's an undeniable aspect of American life and our racial divisions animate much of our political discourse, even if few people will openly admit it.

It's also not true that a rising tide lifts all boats. In fact, studies by the Kirwan Institute and others have shown that stimulus money that was meant to be that rising tide that would lift all boats actually exacerbated racial inequality because those organizations and institutions best able to navigate the political process and get ahold of that money were able to access it. Meanwhile, those most in need were unable to access funds that would help.

Obama does himself and all of us a disservice by not talking openly, honestly, and candidly about our current racial realities and our obligations as Americans to rise to the racial challenges that are presented today, to acknowledge that real racial disparities and inequalities continue to exist, and that we must be aggressive in addressing them.

THREE

Dollars and Sense? Race, Recession, and Recovery

Racial equality and economic parity with Dr. Julianne Malveaux

The economic recession that was officially declared to have ended in June 2009 never really went away. The emotional and financial wounds inflicted on millions by the global economic meltdown that began in 2007 continue to impact the lives American families and individuals. For many, things keep getting worse. In September 2011 the U.S. Bureau of the Census report established that "An additional 2.6 million people slipped below the poverty line in 2010 . . . making 46.2 million people in poverty in the United States, the highest number in the 52 years the Census Bureau has been tracking it, said Trudi Renwick, chief of the Poverty Statistic Branch at the Census Bureau."[20] Few disagree that the recession will continue to dictate the economic landscape long after the 2012 presidential election.

Economists look for glimmers of hope in manufacturing sales, personal income levels, and employment rates, among other factors. But as I write these words with the radio playing in the background, no such optimism can be heard in the voices of the desparate calling in to the station. Caller one: a father forced to house his young family in a car for months. Caller two: a jobless and insuranceless cancer patient is denied food stamps because he receives too much in unemployment benefit. Caller three: a woman speaks of a family member who took his own life to escape the helplessness of long-term unemployment.

Enter President Obama. When he walked through the doors of the White House in January 2009, he inherited a 1.3-trillion-dollar budget deficit, costly wars in Afghanistan and Iraq, nationwide unemployment at 7.6 percent[21] plus a U.S. banking system in crisis. How could he begin to change the nation's financial fortunes and those of black America?

One person who spoke to the economic frustrations of middle-class African Americans was Velma Hart. At a town hall meeting in Philadelphia in September 2010, Ms. Hart said she was "exhausted" at defending Obama, a candidate "who said he was going to change things in a meaningful way for the middle class." Hart said she believed her family was "well beyond the hot-dogs-and-beans-era of our lives" before posing a final question to President Obama: "Is this my new reality?"[22]

Hart's new reality is the status quo for many African Americans who are not part of the middle class. Numbers from the Bureau of the Census show that one in six Americans have sunk into poverty, the worst things have been since 1993. African Americans are the hardest hit, with 25.8 percent of America's black population trying to make ends meet below the poverty line.

Further threats were placed on this new reality during

the August 2011 debt-ceiling crisis. Freshman Tea Party law-makers held fast to their campaign promises to rein in federal government spending. Their actions almost derailed an increase to the 14.3-trillion-dollar limit, without which military salaries, Medicare payments, and other government bills would have gone unpaid. A deal at the eleventh hour was reached, but not without consequences—the downgrade of the U.S. government's AAA credit rating by Standard & Poor's. Some analysts say that the move by S&P could have a negative effect on interest rates for everything from car loans to mortgages, directly impacting ordinary Americans.

No matter how statistics are presented—as colorful pie charts or mind twisting numbers in surveys—it's the people behind the figures that matter. How can the president's message of hope translate into dollars and cents for African Americans?

To address the economics of black Americans, I needed someone who could clear the numerical clutter and get to the heart of the chaos caused by the economic crash.

Dr. Julianne Malveaux is an economist, author, social commentator, and president of Bennett College for Women in North Carolina. Dr. Malveaux has been keeping a watchful eye on Obama's policies and economic smarts and is intent on holding him accountable for his words, actions, and deeds.

Dr. Malveaux's columns on the economy are not always comfortable reading. She blends humanity with complicated statistics on the downturn, moving beyond the racial disparity while being crystal clear about what needs to be done for African Americans economically.

Before analyzing some economic statistics, we began our conversation with her thoughts on Obama.

Julianne: It was unfathomable to me that we would have an African American president so soon, frankly.

As the 2008 election year unfolded, I found myself in what I would call a stunned state of disbelief—joyous disbelief, but disbelief nonetheless. This just did not seem like something that would happen in my lifetime.

Then, of course, as the early results came in, they were much closer than they could have been, but at the same time, states like North Carolina, where Bennett College is located, came through for Obama. It was exhilarating. It was like, "Yes!" You really felt the exhilaration, the joy.

But at the same time, there was a sense of dread about backlash. What does this historic moment mean?

There are various subgroups of people who believe that they "own" Obama. Women, Latinos, young people and African Americans voted for him overwhelmingly. Any subgroup you look at voted for Obama, otherwise, he wouldn't be president. At the same time, that means a lot of people are pulling on his coattails. So what does that mean for a black agenda?

Joanne: What for you *is* the black agenda right now?

Julianne: Well, it's very simple: African American people want social and economic justice. We want the same things other people want. If the unemployment rate is 9.9 percent, we don't want ours to be 16.7 percent. If poverty is 12 percent overall, we don't want our poverty rate to be 25 percent.

Social and economic justice involves people of color and white folks being treated in an evenhanded way, but that hasn't been achieved yet. Whether it's education, health, the economy, housing, jobs—you name it, significant differences continue to persist between black and white Americans. Racial economic gaps simply have not been closed.

At the same time, we still have a significant amount of racial minutia that can rise to the level of racial profiling. Just look at what's happened in Arizona with the passing of the Senate Bill SB1070, some of the most stringent antiimmigration laws in the land. But even more than that, in the same month that Obama was inaugurated as president of the United States, Oakland police shot and killed a black man named Oscar Grant while he was handcuffed and on his knees. No reasonable person can accept the defense that Grant was threatening to the police. The eyewitnesses don't believe that.

The bottom line is that violence of that sort shouldn't happen in the United States anymore, so let's not delude ourselves into thinking that the election of one African American as president of the United States is going to change the world for every African American, especially those at the bottom.

What African American people want is no more than any other American—fair treatment, social and economic justice, an opportunity to achieve and to excel. And those are things that have only been unevenly available.

Joanne: At the Tavis Smiley We Count conference you said you do not want to hear the phrase *post-racial* anymore. Can you expand on that thought?

Julianne: The phrase is utter nonsense. Look at some figures. The overall unemployment rate in April of 2010 was 9.9 percent, but the African American unemployment rate was 16.7 percent. Where is the post-racialism there?

If you look at poverty rates, or income, or anything else, you don't see any post-racialism. Yes, you have people who stepped out of their comfort zone to elect an African American man as president. But consider the alternative. A near octogenarian who babbled his way through the election, paired with somebody who was enormously challenged in dealing with facts?

When you look at it that way, you're surprised that the margin of victory Obama had was not even wider than it was. And you can count on race for some of that.

The post-racial thing is a feel-good phrase. Of course, you have people who are like kids on a long car trip and they ask, "Are we there yet? Are we post-racial yet? Have we gotten there yet?" The goal is to make sure that every American has their contributions and attributes clearly valued. We're *not* there yet and at the rate we're going we're not going to get there anytime soon.

Here's another example. In February 2010, at the University of California at San Diego, a white fraternity threw a "Compton cookout" in honor of Black History Month. Guys were asked to wear Fubu and gold chains, and the women were to dress as "ghetto chicks" and wear bad weaves. The university held a teach-in after this, but these little incidents keep coming up. The Ku Klux Klan is alive and well.

You wouldn't believe the kind of mail I get from time to time, like when I've made comments about the Tea Party. I expect people to disagree with me when I choose to take a controversial position, but they don't need to call me the "N" word.

Post-racial? Nonsense.

Joanne: You wrote in a commentary that President Obama's victory is a moment not a movement. If it is just a moment, what is the movement we're looking for?

Julianne: We're looking at closing gaps. We're looking at access to education. We're looking to economic fairness. We're looking to better distribution.

Dr. Martin Luther King Jr., to whom many liken President Obama, didn't say, "I have a dream that one black man will be president of the United States of America."

When he accepted the Nobel Peace Prize in 1964, he said, "I have the audacity to believe that people everywhere will have three meals a day for their bodies, education and culture for their minds, peace and freedom for their spirits." He talked about people everywhere, not just one black man in the White House.

Now, let me be very, very clear. It would be impossible to minimize the stunning nature of the symbolism of the Obama presidency. This was no symbolic presidency bid in the sense of an Al Sharpton or a Jesse Jackson run. This was a real run, a serious run for the White House—and a successful one. In the world at large, Obama's presidency makes the United States look much greater than we are, much more open than we are.

But have the material conditions for African American people changed because of the Obama Presidency? I would argue that the answer is *no*.

Joanne: Let's talk about the economy. Give us a snapshot of how the economy as it pertains to African Americans today compares with when President Obama took office in January 2009.

Julianne: Well, the unemployment rate is higher. President Obama inherited a very bad economy. The economy was spiralling out of control during the last years of the Bush administration. We were seeing unemployment rates rise to unacceptable territory, and they've continued to rise. I don't blame President Obama for the rise in unemployment, although I do believe that earlier and more frequent intervention could have had impact.

Obama also inherited the mortgage and banking crises, both of which occurred during the Bush years. Henry Paulson, who was then Treasury secretary, went to President Bush and asked for the seven hundred-billion dollar bailout.

So we have to separate these things out. And clearly, when we separate them out, we see that President Obama inherited a horrible situation. He made some decisions about how to sequence recovery. He first went after the TARP funds—the Troubled Asset Relief Program—recovery funds. That was a good thing. President Obama then went after health care, which if ever implemented might be the greatest renegotiation of the social contract since the years of Franklin Roosevelt. At the same time, I think that many would have preferred the president tackle the unemployment issue before the health care issue.

As a result, significant political capital, as well as significant budget space, has been lost to the health care crisis and tackling unemployment has now taken the position of a poor third. Depending on the constituency, others would have had him do other things earlier. I know the Latino community is very disturbed about the fact that immigration reform is not at the top of the chart, especially with the passing of SB1070, the Support Our Law Enforcement and Safe Neighborhoods Act, in Arizona.

Looking at the economy, we had already begun to see the deteriorating mortgage situation. It's gotten worse, of course. But those were progressive things. We had already begun to see the unemployment rate tick up. The fact is that it's just gotten worse. It's not Obama's fault, but given a number of things, I think that there could have been earlier interventions.

Joanne: You say that the state of the economy, for the most part, isn't President Obama's fault, but let's look at some of the things that he has done since he's been in office.

Reading some statistics, eighty-five-million dollars was taken away from historically black universities and colleges. We saw seven hundred-billion dollars given to bailout banks, but yet we've only seen to date around eighteen billion dollars going toward helping people who are still unemployed.

So how do you unpick that? Yes, President Obama inherited a really bad economy, but what steps have been taken since then to try to rectify the situation for all those suffering financially, including the hard-hit African American community?

Julianne: That's a very good point. The eighty-five-million dollars that was taken from historically black colleges in the first-year budget has been restored. Presidents, myself included, lobbied to get that money restored as part of an amendment to the health care legislation that talked about restoring educational funding. So it's going to be restored over the next ten years. Of course, at the same time, you have to ask, why was it ever taken?

The employment legislation is just pathetic, frankly. As you say, $787 billion went to the banking system, yet just $18 billion for unemployment. That's wrong. Also, the conversations around unemployment have been inadequate; even the urban economy summit that was held at the White House with President Obama and Ben Jealous from the NAACP, Marc Morial of the National Urban League, and Al Sharpton for the National Action Network. They had a conversation, but they tiptoed around issues of black unemployment.

Let's assume that in Appalachia, which is home mostly to white people, you ended up with an unemployment rate of 28 percent. It would seem to me that a policy analyst and a caring president would say, "Oh, this problem in Appalachia is so extreme, we've got to do something about it. Granted, the entire country has an unemployment rate of 9.9 percent, but that level of unemployment in Appalachia is something we can't live with. Let's throw some special dollars to Appalachia." That's what I would think would happen.

We have a 28 percent unemployment rate in the African American community if you use the U6 number from the Bureau for Labor Statistics; U6 represents the number of people unemployed and underemployed due to the economy.[23] Yet this crisis in the black community has received scant attention. I think that that's what people are concerned about.

The Obama White House seems unwilling to closely identify with helping the African American community, and certainly the backlash from the Tea Party and others around the minimal things he's done—health care, for example—

suggest that if he pushes too far away from neoconservative positions, it will likely incite enormous backlash.

But if you stand for nothing, you'll fall for anything. I think there's a sense of profound disappointment among African American people about the way this president has been responding.

Joanne: And yet, President Obama needed the black vote during the election. People gave money from their pocket. They went out, they rallied, they campaigned.

But now that President Obama is in the White House, it appears that other groups are being more vocal about having their issues addressed, for example the gay/lesbian/bisexual lobby following the end of the "Don't ask, don't tell" policy. Why have African Americans been reluctant to vocalize their needs during this administration?

Julianne: African American leaders and African American people have tried to give President Obama a break. I think that people look around, they see the criticism he's getting and they don't want to be in the front of a throng of critics.

I would also say that those of us who have been Obama's friendly critics have borne the brunt of crazy accusations. A pro-Obama colleague wrote something critical about the president's selection of Elena Kagan for the U.S. Supreme Court. Yet, on his blog, he got half a dozen really ugly, "Oh, yes. You're an Uncle Tom" and "You don't ever support Obama" comments.

So I think that there is a reluctance to be critical, but the organized leadership ought to be more vocal. When you talk about a black agenda, people need to have a ten-point program. This is what we need. We need programs on jobs, we need programs on education. There needs to be more regular meetings with the president. But I don't expect President Barack Obama to call up the NAACP leadership and say, "Yo, what's up? Let's sit down and kick it." I don't think that's ever going to happen.

Part of the challenge is that the relationship between President Obama and the black community reveals the weaknesses in African American leadership. You don't see the same thing with the gay and lesbian community, with the Latino community. People are going and asking for what they want, and they're clear about it. African Americans are not doing that.

Joanne: You touched on the role of black leadership and the need for black leadership to step up. What are the stumbling blocks for black leadership? Why aren't we seeing the baton pass from the civil rights movement through the black power movement to now? Why do we seem to be faltering right now when, in many respects, we have more power than ever? Or perhaps we just think that we have more power?

Julianne: That's such a good question, but I don't think batons are ever formally passed. I think that there are some younger leaders who have been very disparaging of older leaders and want them to get out of the way so they can ascend to the stage. Well, you don't ascend; leadership is not like peanuts at a cocktail party. You don't say, "Pass the leadership; I'd like some." It's something that's really earned. If you think you're leading and nobody is following you, then you're not leading; you're just tripping.

We have some veteran leaders who I would not remove from the stage if you paid me. Rev. Jesse Jackson brings phenomenal wisdom to the table. The late Dorothy Irene Height brought true insight every day.

The question becomes: how does a Jackson coexist with a Ben Jealous from the NAACP or a Marc Morial from the National Urban League or an Al Sharpton? How do these men of very different generations—Jackson seventy, Sharpton and Morial mid-fifties, Jealous late thirties—share power, coexist, correlate, or divide up the policy space, which is huge, so that people are in areas of specialty? And most importantly, at a policy moment where it seems there is more possibility than ever, how do we maximize it without degenerating into ineffectiveness?

Joanne: You talked about the black leadership being better coordinated. Why the lack of coordination currently?

Julianne: When you've operated in a small space on a small scale, there tends to be a lot of clashing egos. The challenge is ego management. Knowing when to shine and when to sit down; when it's time to step up, when it's time to take a position, when it's time to let someone else take the position. Both Bush administrations and Reagan's White House were hostile environments for African Americans. You operate differently in a hostile environment than you do in a friendly one.

At least the Obama administration is clearly being friendly to African American people. But that's not enough.

Joanne: What about women who are the decision makers? You talked before about Dr. Dorothy Height. Why are we not seeing more people, more women like the late Dr. Height involved in the leadership process, whether it be at the governmental level or at the community level?

Julianne: When I look at African American women's leadership, I'm not looking at the Obamas. I'm looking at our civil rights organizations and asking why we've never had a woman lead the NAACP. Or why the Urban League has never focused on African American women as leaders. Or why so many of our civil rights organizations have not believed in cogendered leadership. It's a really huge question in the African American community. We have some unaddressed sexism, and some male privilege that, again, remains unaddressed. There's this notion that African American women are supposed to step aside because men are accustomed to doing the leading.

This clearly isn't the case for everyone and, certainly, when I look around, there are people such as Melanie Campbell who leads the Black Women's Roundtable, a part of the National Coalition on Black Civic Participation. When we look at the list of the women who participate in that group, you've got some real firepower, women who can organize and who do great work. So the issue also becomes why the media and others tend to focus more on the work that men do and less on that of women.

For example, after Don Imus made the very unfortunate comments about African American women in sports, MSNBC asked me to comment on the story. The hour-long program began with a bunch of white men defending Imus, followed by Rev. Jackson and Marc Morial from the Urban League. I was sitting in the studio and I finally said to them,

"If it's time for me to leave, I'll go." In a conversation about women, my woman's voice got two minutes at the end of the hour. I sat there for the whole time while the show was produced for men to dominate. When I spoke up about this, the anchor at the time said, "Well, you know, Rev. Jackson is better known than you are."

The mainstream media does not mind lifting up black conservatives. Anytime they bring on a liberal, they're going to also find a conservative. So why not use the same kind of logic and invite women to the table?

Joanne: Away from the leaders, let's talk wealth in this country. Why is there still such a disparity between the wealth of races in the United States and where do African Americans stack up within that?

Julianne: The best way to describe the wealth situation is to use the words of Lauryn Hill. "It's not what you got, it's what you keep." In other words, earnings are one thing. What you keep, what you invest in is another.

African Americans, on average, earn about 60 percent of what whites earn. So the opportunity to keep is far narrower than it is for white Americans. In addition, after generations of unequal pay, black families have less wealth to pass on by way of inheritance than do white families.

In education, African American students take on more loans, so their opportunities to accumulate wealth are deferred by their need to pay off the debts incurred by their education.

Income is a snapshot. It's what you have today. To put it another way, wealth is also like a history lesson—it's what you *haven't* gotten all this time.

So, while I think the numbers are stark, I don't think they're surprising. For example, the Insight Center for Community Economic Development's spring 2010 report on the wealth gap between women of color and white women states that an unmarried woman of color between the ages of thirty-six and forty-nine has an average wealth of *five dollars*, compared with over *forty-two thousand dollars* for an unmarried white woman in the same age range.[24]

Joanne: Five dollars?

Julianne: Five dollars.

Joanne: You can't really do anything with five dollars.

Julianne: Exactly. Well, that's the average, so half above, half below. But what does that mean? On the one hand, you say, "Oh, my; that's a horrible statistic." On the other hand, if these are moms that are taking care of children, sending them to college, dealing with their challenges, feeding them, clothing them, etcetera, when do they have an opportunity to save, even for their own pensions? In this context, the income piece is like your midterm exam, but the wealth piece is like the semester report card; your GPA for the whole four years you're in college, to use an analogy.

So the wealth data are troubling, but they really speak to the different infusions that the African American, Latino, White, and Asian communities have had into their earnings. You have differences in home ownership rates up until five years ago, since then home ownership has been one of the ways that communities have been able to grow wealth.

Again, think about it. If African Americans did not own homes at the same rate that whites did, they had less opportunities. And again, why was that? We can go back and look at the history of redlining at the Federal Home Administration and the ways they wrote legislation in the 1930s that provided whites with subsidized mortgages but prevented African Americans from getting them.

You can also look to World War II and the post–World War II era. There's a book out called *When Affirmative Action Was White: An Untold History of Racial Inequality in Twentieth-Century America* by Ira Katznelson that describes how African Americans who fought in World War II did not get the same federal dollars to buy homes or to attend college and to move from working class to professional. Most white soldiers did.

Black men who wanted to use the GI Bill to improve themselves were restricted to between six and ten weeks of training, while whites got four years of college. So all of that shows up in the wealth statistics.

Joanne: Staying with the situation for women, so often, with the unemployment figures in particular, we get a sense of how tough things are for African American men, but from an economic standpoint, what is the situation for women?

Julianne: African American women are facing major economic challenges. While our unemployment rate is a little bit lower than that of African American men, it's certainly much higher than that of white women.

Many people are calling the recession a *mancession* because men are experiencing more layoffs than women are. But

African American women are finding a whole array of challenges because of their occupational concentration. Those pursuing professional and managerial careers are doing better than those who are in clerical and service positions, but all of these workers are getting squeezed.

African American women disproportionately work for governments. And so, as governments have budget cuts, that affects African American women. You have people who are working fewer hours who also are more vulnerable to the possibility of layoffs.

In addition, African American women are more likely than other women to be single moms and be heads of households. More than 40 percent of African American households are headed by black women, and many of these women are the only means of support for their children.

Joanne: So what policies need to be put in place to make things better for African American women?

Julianne: The whole issue of childcare—affordable childcare—is very important. Addressing employment discrimination is also very important. When we're looking at federal jobs and state jobs, the issue of how layoffs are distributed is crucial for African American women. Housing discrimination against African American women is another core issue. These are all areas we should pay attention to.

Then there's a concept I call "the third burden" of African American women. We have the burden of race, we have the burden of gender, but the unequal economic treatment of African American men also has an impact on African American women. If a woman has children with a man who has been economically marginalized, that puts a greater economic burden on her. How is that burden to be dealt with?

When we look at education, African American women represent two-thirds of our nation's African American undergraduates. African American women are more likely than African American men to go to college. Many will say, "Well, gee, let's pay more attention to the men," and certainly we do want to close that gap because it has long-term implications for community development and family formation.

Joanne: We're also still looking at the impact of the subprime loan debacle and the crisis of foreclosures with which so many Americans have been hit. How can people who have lost their homes begin to crawl out from under that while the costs of food, gas, and living continue to rise?

Julianne: The situation is turning out poorly. The gaps are widening, not closing, even though the whole housing crisis has had a differential impact. Renters are also being hit. If you are renting from someone who defaulted on their mortgage, you might find yourself homeless even though you haven't missed a rental payment. You see a lot of that in the inner cities. African Americans are being hit really hard there. And again, we haven't really talked about race-specific strategies to deal with some of this. For me, this is where the biggest challenges lie.

Joanne: And why has there not been more race-specific action when it's been proven time and time again that if there's a problem that pertains to a particular community, if you target it, it can be solved more efficiently?

Julianne: People in the United States are generally uncomfortable talking about race. This is especially true when it comes to policy. When you begin to talk about race from a policy perspective, people just cringe. They step back. They don't want to talk about it.

Many people thought that the Obama presidency would have made it easier for Americans to deal with race matters, but things are not turning out that way at all. In some ways, it has become more difficult. You have people who say things like, "We're post-racial. We're over racism. Just get over it."

And yet, even if you got over it emotionally and if you got over it from a policy perspective, you still have report cards, like the Wealth Data, that suggests you can "get over it" by never referring to it and that means that you have chosen to accept a substandard place in the economic spectrum.

Joanne: At the 2010 We Count event, you shared a quote regarding an exchange between Franklin Roosevelt and civil rights activist A. Philip Randolph. Roosevelt said to him, "You want change? Make me; push me." What or who is pushing President Obama to address African American concerns?

Julianne: That's the most forceful question: who's going to push him and who's going to make him? And how is it done so that everybody walks away feeling clean, so that it's done without being an attack?

I don't think a strategy has been fully developed in this regard. You have too many African Americans who have been very eager to approach the Obama administration saying, "Oh, you don't have to deal with those radicals. Just deal with me."

You have people who are getting access to the president on the basis of their willingness to basically mute dissent. But the dissent has to bubble up. Obama can be great. I think he has so much going for him. He's extraordinarily intelligent, he's a great communicator, he's a bridge builder. There's a lot that he can do. But he's got to feel as passionate about having strong black support as he does about having strong Jewish, Latino, gay and lesbian, or any other kind of support.

And until he feels that strongly, he's going to be able to do whatever he wants to do and you're going to have people who are going to say to him, "It's not going to matter." Where else are they going to go? Are they going to vote for Republicans?

Well, the answer is no. People aren't going to vote for Republicans. They'll probably just stay home.

Joanne: Glen Ford from the *Black Agenda Report* put together a report on President Obama's performance during his first hundred days in office, looking at everything from health care reform, new jobs, and preserving public education and so forth. As an academic, give us your report card on President Obama so far. How's he doing?

Julianne: Well, he's not failing. I think he gets like a low B; a low B or a medium B. There's no A+, there's no A-. It's not in the excellent range. I think he's done good work. He has not failed miserably on anything. I think he's honing a style that is a style I actually like.

When he puts his hand on public policy, I think we see a difference. I think we saw that with the health care debate, but it took time, and the right wing continues to push back viciously against it. So you have to put your leader hat on and go in there. But in the medium run, he seems to be okay. I give him either a B- or an incomplete.

Joanne: How likely is it that he will be reelected, in your opinion?

Julianne: I think it's very possible. The question people are going to ask in 2012 is the Reagan question: Are you better off now than you were four years ago? If the economy comes back a little quicker than we think it might, it's possible for him to win.

If health care has been phased in and people don't see huge jumps in their premiums, that will help him win their vote. If the unemployment is 7 percent and not 9, that will also help him win. He has to be very strategic about it, though, and time is running out.

FOUR

Barack Obama: The New Crack?

A Story of Revolution with Ramona Africa

May 13, 1985: A bomb explodes on the home of black revolutionaries in Philadelphia. Six adults and five children were killed that day and sixty-one homes razed to the ground. The order to drop the bomb was given by a black man, Mayor Willie Wilson Goode.

This is the story of the MOVE Organization: a family of activists brought together by common beliefs in natural law, self-defenses, and the value of all life. Founded by John Africa in 1972, MOVE members were an object of curiosity for the public and a menace in the eyes of local law enforcement officers.

In 1978, MOVE was ordered to vacate the organization's headquarters in Powelton Village. The mandate led to a year-long standoff that ended with gunfire. Seven years of tension followed, this time ending with the police bombing MOVE members while they were inside a building. Two people survived the attack: Ramona Africa and a young boy named Birdie.

Ramona Africa openly defines herself as a revolutionary. The courage of her convictions are palpable; the pain of the past not far below the surface, although the power in her voice would lead the casual listener to think otherwise.

Throughout our conversation, in part personal biography and a call to action, Ramona implores every individual to take responsibility for the change they wish to see, her desire realized in small part by the anti–Wall Street demonstrations which started in September 2011.

Ramona's story is one of many that illustrate the brutality faced by those called to confront and fight against the social and political injustices experienced in black America. More than twenty-five years after the fateful police attacks that killed her brothers and sisters in struggle, Ramona Africa is about her mission: to tell the story of the revolutionaries who dare to live outside of the norms of American society. What happens to them? How do they get by? What does the notion of black leadership and an African American president mean in their eyes?

Ramona: I'm Ramona Africa. I'm minister of communication for the MOVE Organization. I was a former political prisoner of seven years, and I am the sole adult survivor of the police bombing of the MOVE Organization that took place in May 1985. I am also a representative of the International Concerned Family and Friends of Mumia Abu-Jamal. But most importantly, I am a revolutionary.

Joanne: You define yourself as a revolutionary, and that is where I'd like to start, Ramona, with definitions. I interviewed Dr. Vincent Harding at the beginning of this project;

he was a speechwriter for Dr. Martin Luther King Jr. and himself an activist and a scholar.

We began our conversation talking about the civil rights movement and he said, "No, we have to look at the definition." So with each person I've interviewed since then, I've asked them to define what it is that they do, as opposed to the definitions and labels enforced by the media and others. How would you define and describe MOVE?

Ramona: As I define myself, MOVE is a revolutionary organization and by *revolution*, some people interpret that to mean bloody confrontation. That is not how MOVE interprets revolution. Revolution simply means change. It means to activate, to generate, and that is our mission.

We live under the thumb of a system that cares absolutely nothing—less than nothing—about life, about anything that's alive. Our belief is exactly the opposite. John Africa, MOVE's founder, teaches that there is absolutely nothing more important than life, that life must be the priority. Not *a* priority, *the* priority.

When we say *life*, we're not talking about life in an abstract hug-a-tree sense. We're talking about the seriousness of all life, without category.

Joanne: How did you become involved in MOVE?

Ramona: I came from a fairly middle-class black family. I was raised by my mother. She's a beautician by trade. I went to Catholic school from first to twelfth grade. I worked for approximately one year after I graduated high school; I had a so-called good job with benefits and all that. I really didn't know, personally, about injustices and brutality. I did, however, read various books and I did know about people like the Black Panthers and Malcolm X. I knew a little something even about MOVE.

During my last year at Temple University, I got a work-study job with Community Legal Service, a free state-sponsored legal aid society active here in Philadelphia and throughout Pennsylvania.

My first day of work was August 8, 1978, and the office I had to report to was in north Philadelphia, but my supervisor was having me work as a volunteer with a tenant action group. As my supervisor and I were driving from north Philadelphia to Center City we listened to an all-news radio station give a blow-by-blow account of the police attack on MOVE. We were horrified. When I got to the office I continued to tune in to the coverage of what was happening. That's really as far as it went then. But, working in housing, I soon became an activist, because you cannot work for tenants and organize tenants without becoming active.

I would go to city council with a local activist named Milton Street; he would have his supporters shout down city council members, demanding housing and justice for tenants. I started going over there with him and I ended up getting arrested in city council. That was my first arrest. It was no big deal.

At my first court date I met a young man named Mel. We exchanged numbers and he called me one day and asked if I wanted to go to a meeting to plan a MOVE demonstration. I guess it was just time. We went to the meeting that night and I met some long-time MOVE supporters. I met my sister Pam Africa and she started telling me a lot of things about MOVE that I didn't know; she gave me some MOVE material to read—some of the writings of John Africa—and encouraged me to go over to city hall and sit in on the MOVE trials and see for myself what was going on in the courtroom.

When I sat in that courtroom, I could not believe what I was seeing; it was absolutely nothing like what I was reading in textbooks or what those professors were telling me at Temple University as to how the legal system or the court system operates.

I saw railroading. I saw racism. I also saw a group of young people representing themselves in court—MOVE people—not intimidated at all, expertly exposing the lies and inconsistencies in the prosecution witnesses, and I was impressed.

I kept going back to court. Then I started going up to the prison to visit them and talk to them personally. This was the MOVE 9, the people who were arrested on August 8, 1978, and were serving thirty to one hundred years in jail.

Joanne: They were the ones accused of killing Officer James Ramp during the gunfire at the MOVE headquarters in Powelton Village.

Ramona: Yes. The more I went to court to visit them, the more I became identified by the cops and officials as a MOVE supporter. As a result, they started targeting me. I ended up getting arrested again because the judge barred me from the trial. From that point forward, when I went to trial, I represented myself like MOVE people. Judge Lynne Abraham, who later became the district attorney, found me guilty of whatever it was they were charging me with—disorderly conduct, disrupting a governmental function, something like that.

On the day of my sentencing, she asked me if I had anything to say. "Yes," I said, and I began describing what I had seen in that courtroom during the MOVE trials and who the real criminal was. She told me to shut up, and I said, "Well, didn't you just ask me if I had anything to say? And isn't this supposed to be America where there's freedom of speech and freedom of religion and freedom of the press and all of these freedoms?" She said, "No," and sentenced me to sixty days contempt of court, sixty days in prison.

What she had not taken into account was that she was sending me to the county jail for sixty days to live up close and personal with MOVE women. When that sixty-day contempt sentence was up and I was released, I was more committed than ever. There was nothing anybody could say to lessen my determination.

So, it was Judge Lynne Abraham that kicked me right into MOVE. It was the best thing she ever could have done for me.

Joanne: How do you feel that MOVE fits in with other elements of black empowerment, the traditional civil rights movement, the black power movement, and so on?

Ramona: Because John Africa taught total revolution, there are aspects of MOVE that fit in with organizations across the board. Militant organizations like the Panthers, or Us, or SNCC; animal rights organizations, environmental organizations, health-conscious organizations, the movement for home birthing, and so on.

There are also obstacles that we have to overcome because, for example, there's this new Black Panther organization, and they consider themselves militant. Organizations like that embrace the militant side of MOVE, but they don't express solidarity with us when we demonstrate at the zoo against the enslavement and abuse of animals.

They're like, "What are you wasting your time on that for? We've got people that have been in jail thirty, forty years, brothers and sisters." We're like, "How can anyone complain about their being in jail and yet sanction the lion, the bear, all these other animals being in jail for life?"

Either you believe in freedom or you don't. The instant you make an allowance for enslavement and abuse, then you don't believe in freedom.

Joanne: Talking of animal freedom also leads us to discussing the environment and caring for the planet. How do you feel that green politics and green policies have been addressed thus far? Van Jones, President Obama's former green adviser spoke about this also.

Ramona: It's a contradiction in terms. You can't believe in politics and this system, period, particularly this capitalist system, and believe in the environment as well. It's a contradiction in terms. It's a clash.

Joanne: Why do you say that?

Ramona: Because if you're talking about the environment—cleaning it up and putting things right, getting rid of pollution and poison—you're talking about getting rid of corporate

America. There is not one politician on the face of this earth that is prepared to do that or work toward that because it's not something that would happen overnight.

So, it's nothing but a trick, a front. It's nothing but talk when these politicians, including Obama, discuss the environment and green living. It's a new phase, a popular position to take, and it's bull. They don't really mean it.

When then–Senator Obama first decided to run, people would come up to MOVE, especially black people, and say, "Oh, I know you're going to vote for Obama, he can make history as the first black president. What do you think about Obama?" I said, "Well, he's a politician." "Yeah, but what do you think about him?" "Well, he's a politician. That tells you everything you need to know. He's a politician and he's going to do what is politically favorable for himself."

People said, "Well, I know you're going to vote for Obama. He's going to be the first black president." I said, "Yeah. It's the same thing people said about Wilson Goode. Vote for him; he'll be the first black mayor. And look what he did."

Joanne: Wilson Goode was the mayor Philadelphia who gave the order to drop the bomb on the MOVE headquarters in 1985.

Ramona: The building he bombed was our home.

Joanne: You expressed your thoughts very clearly; President Obama is a politician. Do you or MOVE believe anything changed with the election of an African American president? Did you vote?

Ramona: No, we don't believe in voting, but I'll tell you exactly what I think.

I was with Fred Hampton Jr. recently. He said, "Barack Obama is the new crack. He has anesthetized people, got people hallucinating. He's the new crack in the black community and poor communities."

Joanne: Powerful words. A theme that has developed with almost everyone I've interviewed for this project is that black people are reluctant to hold President Obama accountable, which may speak a little to Fred Hampton Jr.'s thoughts that he's "the new crack."

Ramona: Yes. That situation with Skip Gates, the Harvard professor who was a friend of Obama's.

Joanne: You're talking about Professor Henry Louis Gates, the one whose neighbor called the police as he was trying to get into his own house.

Ramona: If the only thing that Obama could do in response to a situation like that is invite Gates and the cop to the White House for a beer, then that is a sad commentary. Initially, I believe Obama said, "There was no excuse for what happened." Then whoever is pulling his strings must have asked him what he thought he was doing and got him to back off. The next thing you know, he was inviting them to the White House for a beer.

So if he can't even speak out forcefully and honestly about a situation like that—and Gates is the president's friend—what do people think he's going to do for them as black people?

Joanne: Do you think he should be doing more specifically for African Americans?

Ramona: I think he should be doing more for everybody, but I also know that he can't. He absolutely can't.

Joanne: Why do you think he can't?

Ramona: Because, first of all, he is beholden to those who put him in office. Second of all, he's a politician. If you think that this one term as president of the United States is the end of his political aspirations, you're wrong. He's not going to cut off his nose to spite his face. And he's just one person; he can't do what needs to be done.

People have to stop looking for a savior. There is no savior out there. We, the people, are our own saviors. We have to be. And until we stop looking for somebody to come down from the heavens and wave a magic wand and make everything all right, until we stop looking for that and get up off our butts and start working ourselves to put things right, then nothing is ever going to get better.

Joanne: Has that been a downfall of organizations like SNCC, the black power movement, the traditional civil rights move-ment—have African Americans been too quick to look for, as you say, a savior, a messiah, that quick fix representative?

Ramona: Absolutely, but not just black folks, everyone. Eve-ryone is a victim of this because external government exists all over the world. People abdicate responsibility for themselves and think they can give it to somebody else to take care of.

It's a violation. It's a crime. It's wrong. We're not going to get anything good or right out of that.

Can anybody eat and fill your stomach? Can somebody else drink and quench your thirst? If I run ten minutes a day, is that going to put muscle on your legs? It can't. The same principle applies. You cannot abdicate responsibility for yourself. You cannot give your power of purpose to somebody else. The only time that you are supposed to be responsible for another being is when you become a parent, then you are responsible for your children until they become equipped to take care of themselves. Other than that, nobody else is responsible for you.

That is the problem with cops, judges, politicians, prison guards, all of these officials of authority—it's unnatural to have that kind of authority over another human being, particularly adult human beings. And because it's a violation, it messes with your thinking, with your mentality, and it gives people a god-complex.

Joanne: Do you think that the various movements and agents for social change led to us having an African American president, or do you believe it was a moment in time, that this was going to happen anyway?

Ramona: I think at some point it would have happened. People are getting more and more dissatisfied and disillusioned as the economy goes down the tubes, even with people that have money who feel like they've done everything right.

To me, it was a strategic move to put Obama in at this time because it did just what those in authority wanted him to do; anesthetized people, diverted people, and made people feel like it's a brand new day in America. Imagine, the first black president of the United States! People were going crazy about this. Now, it hasn't taken long for people to start going the other way, seeing that nothing has really changed for them.

Joanne: So in your opinion, who drove this agenda to get a black man in the White House?

Ramona: There are a handful of the super rich that really run the world, not just America, but the world; they decide what's going to happen. I don't know how anybody at this point can hallucinate that going behind a curtain and pulling a lever is what helps communities, helps the environment, or causes the kind of change we all want. Didn't Florida in 2000 teach people anything? Decision making has nothing to do with voting.

Joanne: So you think that African Americans didn't actually have much of a say, so to speak, when it came to electing President Obama?

Ramona: Once they put Obama out there, I think they knew that the African American community was going to go crazy and all out for him. I mean, it was amazing.

If people would use one-half of the energy they used to get Obama elected for themselves, it would be a brand new day here in America.

Joanne: You said that people on the street assumed that MOVE members would vote for Obama in the 2008 election. How did they respond when you said, "I'm not going to vote"?

Ramona: They said, "Oh, why you gotta come down on the brother? Give the brother a chance!" I just said, "Look, don't worry about me. You go on and do what you've got to do. Time will tell it all."

People have said the same thing about Wilson Goode and other black elected officials over time. First black elected governor, congressman, senator. You've got more black elected officials than ever and you've got more crime, more police brutality, more poor people, more suffering today than ever before. Where are the benefits of this? I'm trying to see it and I don't see it.

Joanne: We talked before about legacy, about people being responsible for themselves, for their community and what they do. A lot of people will look at some of the traditional movement activists, like Fannie Lou Hamer, for example, who was beaten and jailed in order to give people the right to vote, to allow them to have their say at the ballot box.

You say that voting doesn't make any difference; how, then, do we start to change society, change America for African Americans if we're not going to do it at the ballot box?

Ramona: John Africa taught that the change, the revolution, starts inside you. It starts with the way you think and the way you live. It is that example that influences those closest to you; your mate, your children, your family members, then those extended family members and neighbors. That is how you change.

Things did not get to the degenerated state they are to-day overnight. It was a very gradual, long-term process. And it's not going to be cleared up overnight. There is no quick fix.

As we start changing the way we think, we start changing things around us; that's the way parents influence their children and instill in them the commitment to live and work and relate to the world and others in new ways. That is what changes things, not pulling a lever or a busload of hope in elected politicians.

I know that people are not just going to stop voting and I'm not telling people to stop voting. But I am saying that if you believe in voting and in these politicians, fine, go on out there, vote, but don't leave it at that.

When there are issues in your family, in your community, get in those politicians' faces and remind them of their job, their duty, and the promises they made when they were running. That's what pushes them. It will then become very clear to those politicians that they're not going to be able to just go out there and get your vote, get in office, and live the high life; that people are going to be on their butts about it. That's going to cut down on the number of people that are going to want those positions after a while.

Joanne: You've spoken with thousands of people around the world, but let's bring it back to the United States: when you tell your story and talk about activism and being active in social change, what reasons do people give for not engaging in the process?

Ramona: Well, I think there are a number of reasons. President Obama, he is one reason. Another reason is that people respond to crises. People will suffer as long as they can take it before fighting back and responding.

Another reason is the economy. People are so bogged down with trying to put the next meal on the table, trying to pay their rent, trying to find a job and just survive, that the thought of going to a meeting, a demonstration, or anything else feels like too much to deal with.

I understand that, but people have to also understand that the things that they are complaining about, the things that are putting all this pressure on them, are not going to go away until they get involved and do what's necessary to get the system off their back.

Then you have a group of people who feel like the system is working for them, who feel like they've got a little nest egg, they've got a nice little house, a car. Their kids are in college and they feel like the system is working for them, until it all falls apart.

So, I think it's a lot of things. And then you have the people that think things are crazy, the system is wrong, but MOVE will take care of it. We get phone calls all the time. "My son was just killed by the cops and I know you know how to deal with such things."

They call us. We're not a social service agency and we can't do people's work for them. We will talk to people. We will give them some advice, but it's like people think we're politicians, that they can call us and we'll take care of it, and we just can't.

We can be an example and we can support them, but we can't do people's fighting for them.

Joanne: And that brings us back a point your raised earlier:

people taking responsibility for their own lives and communities and not looking to organizations or individuals, to be the Messiah and to fill the gap.

Ramona: People that have the spotlight, the Jesse Jacksons, the Al Sharptons, and so on, they have a responsibility to use their positions to speak out strongly and forcefully on issues. If they have that limelight, then they do have a responsibility to use it the right way.

I'll give you an example. Jesse Jackson came to Philadelphia in 1995, when Mumia Abu-Jamal had a post-conviction hearing before the trial judge, Albert Sabo. Jesse Jackson came here amongst a flutter of media attention and one journalist said, "You're out here in support of Mumia Abu-Jamal. Have you read the transcripts?" And all Jesse Jackson could say was, "No, I haven't read the transcripts." Instead of saying, "No, I have not read the transcripts from Mumia's trial, but I'm a black man living in America and I know what happens every day. I don't have to read transcripts to find out what happened. I live it."

So, what impression did that give? It says he was just out here on the bandwagon. That behavior does not help anything at all, not then and not now. As a leader, you're not going to know what's happening with every single case going on, but you don't have to. All you have to have is common sense and a loyalty to the people and be able to express that. Other than that, you're doing a disservice to the people.

Joanne: So, what is the way forward? As a revolutionary, what are the next steps?

If voting isn't enough, if leaders, either self-appointed or otherwise, aren't stepping up and using the microphone in a responsible way, then what is the next step, in your opinion?

Ramona: People have to make a decision, have to make up their minds. Do they want to be safe, free, happy and satisfied? Or do they want to continue to live under the thumb of a system that has robbed them of everything—their health, parenthood, happiness, satisfaction, contentment, their freedom, justice, equality? What do people want?

They're going to have to come to grips with this and make a decision as to what's important to them, what their priority is and that has to be done on an individual person-by-person basis. And people are going to have to set the example themselves to show what it is they want and believe in and are working for. Mere voting has never and will never achieve what getting involved accomplishes.

There is no easy way out. It takes work. It takes commitment. It takes loyalty. I'm sorry, there's no magic wand. And that is the only thing that is going to change things. If people want to keep on voting, that's their business. But I'm simply saying it's not the solution. It's not enough to improve our condition for us.

And this is for everybody because when I say improve our condition, I'm not just talking about stopping police brutality; I'm talking about your health too. Everyone's got to breathe the air. Everyone's got to drink the water; rich, poor, black, white, woman, man, old, young, everyone.

Nobody is exempt from this work, and the more people try to run from it and prolong it the more we prolong our own suffering. So people have a decision to make and the work of a revolutionary is to inform people with strong revolutionary information and set a strong revolutionary example to back up the information.

Joanne: Bearing in mind what you say about revolutionary commitment being about benefiting everybody, do you feel that the various factions of the black freedom movement had the emphasis wrong? Should the effort have looked toward improvement for all, as opposed to just African Americans?

Ramona: I won't say it was wrong or barking up the wrong tree. I do understand, based on my belief, that unless you're talking about equality and freedom and justice across the board, then you're not going to get anywhere.

At the same time, I do understand that people are oppressed, like black people in this country are, of course. We're obligated to speak out about our particular condition, our particular situation and work to improve that, but it needs to be in conjunction with overall freedom, justice, equality.

The condition of black people in this country, particularly during the civil rights movement, was really bad. So of course, this particular group of people—black people, African Americans—were going to focus on what they were experiencing. Absolutely.

So I don't see that as wrong. I just see that it has to be in conjunction with the principle of freedom across the board or else it's not going to work.

Joanne: If you had an opportunity to sit down with some of America's black leadership and President Obama today, what are the issues you would put on the table and what advice, in some respects, would you give to President Obama about how to move forward with the revolution as you see it, in terms of improvements to the economy, health-care, and the green agenda?

Ramona: Well, I think you're talking about an exercise in futility because these leaders, Obama particularly, have an agenda, and what MOVE is working for—our belief and direction—are all moving in the opposite direction of where they are trying to take us.

Obama would probably listen politely and that would be the end of it because they have political aspirations. They're not talking about letting this system go. They're not talking about moving away from this system that is the root of every single problem existing. They're talking about perpetuating it and holding onto it, keeping it afloat. And that's completely opposite to MOVE's work.

We're telling people that the only solution is to let this system go because as long as it exists, you are going to have all of the problems that you complain about. As long as you have police, you're going to have police brutality. You're going to have it. And to think that you could do certain things to stop it is futile.

From the invention of the car or the plane, there has been one problem after the other; one so-called improvement after the other. But there are still crashes, aren't there? Because it can't be improved or made safe. As long as they exist, there are going to be problems like crashes and people killed.

So, the same applies with this system. As long as it exists, you are going to have these problems that people, all of us, complain about. The only solution is when we let this system go and live as life dictates, because we humans think that we are the superior beings, that we can conquer nature, that we can make things work in spite of mother nature and the way she has things coordinated. But all humans have done is wreak havoc all over the world.

Joanne: Why do you stay? I was speaking to a colleague very recently who is working on a project called "If You Don't Like It, Leave," the premise being that for African Americans there is a better way of living in another country rather than putting up with a lot of the stuff that happens in the United States. Why do you and the other members of MOVE choose to stay in the United States when you would probably be treated with far more respect and received more openly elsewhere, in Africa for example?

Ramona: Because this is where the work needs to be. Other countries that live simpler, more naturally, they don't need all the work! We're about solutions, and solutions mean being where the problems are.

You can't run from it. You can't go isolate yourself off on some nice little tropical island or anywhere else for that matter. If you want things to be better, you have to do the work to make it better. You have to apply a solution and work to apply the solution.

So we're where the problem is and we intend to do the work to set an example to solve the problem. And for us, not just for anybody else, but for ourselves and our children, that's why we keep doing this work. That's why, despite all we've been through, we continue to do this work because it's for me. Very selfishly. I'm, first and foremost, I'm doing this for me as opposed to anybody else because I need to feel satisfied with myself that I'm doing what's right, that I'm refusing to accept wrong.

Again, the most important thing to do is just keep doing our work, keep setting a strong example, keep that strong revolutionary information out there. It's gradual. It's definitely not as quick as we would like to see things happen. But things are moving. Things are definitely moving.

FIVE

Probing the President: The Media's Paralysis of Analysis?

Race, the Press, and the White House with Linn Washington Jr.

The media's the most powerful entity on earth. They have the power to make the innocent guilty and to make the guilty innocent, and that's power. Because they control the minds of the masses.—Malcolm X, 1963

Journalists are human and come complete with personal preferences, bias, and worldviews that can, and often do, creep into the news agenda. In a twenty-four-hour news world where image and sound bites reign supreme, the thoughts and decisions of the journalist can have powerful influence on the shaping of public views for those who do not read, listen, and watch widely to form their own independent opinions.

To retain this power, today's media are fighting a never-ending wave of battles. Just as the latest recession placed a monetary stranglehold on a diverse array of industries, so too did the long arm of the economic downturn begin to squeeze the lifeblood out of the press. Sharp declines in advertising revenue for newspapers[25] has forced decades-old publications such as the *Seattle Post-Intelligencer* to reimagine their existence. It's also led to visitations from the grim reaper of layoffs at the *New York Times* and *LA Times*.

Advances in technology place an added burden on the news industry. Media outlets have been forced to offer free content online while fending off competition from niche publications filling in the gaps of mainstream news operations. After all, why pay for a newspaper when the content inside may be old news by the time you sit down to read it? The immediacy of Internet-driven electronic media not only poses a threat to print, but television and radio as well.

Social networking is one of the most powerful game changers in today's news landscape. Information is increasingly percolated through online communities and the social media hubs of Facebook, Twitter, and Google+. People now have the power to curate their own radio and TV stations via podcasts and video-hosting sites such as YouTube and Hulu, allowing them to tune in at their leisure; an appointment to view is no longer required.

Yet even with these current challenges and changes, traditional media retain a powerful seat at the table of U.S. society, as enshrined in the United States Constitution.[26]

But as comic Bill Maher once said, "We have the Bill of Rights. What we need is a Bill of Responsibilities."

Veteran journalist Linn Washington Jr. has many concerns about the way media professionals execute their responsibilities. With a career spanning thirty years investigating legal wrongs against African Americans, in our conversation Washington questions the media's analysis of the workings of government and the coverage of race, racism, and the African

American experience. A graduate of the Yale School of Law, Washington teaches journalism as an associate professor at Temple University, exercising the minds of the next generation of media makers and content creators. Linn Washington Jr. doesn't teach in a vacuum. His detailed columns are regularly published in the *Philadelphia Tribune*, the longest continually running African American newspaper in the nation, dating back to 1884.

With a background steeped in the workings of the press, to Washington's mind, the media has two responsibilities, "to provide an informational role, so we would have an informed electorate to help propel and protect and preserve democracy. The other purpose is that of the watchdog. The United States is founded on a system of checks and balances. Who's going to check the checkers?"

With the Obama administration, the relationship between the White House and the media has made headlines in journalism circles. Discussions abound throughout the African American press about the rights and wrongs of criticizing President Obama. Mainstream journalists have focused instead on the reduced access to the White House machine.

According to Towson University political scientist and presidential media interaction analyst Martha Kumar, President Obama held short question-and-answer sessions with the media 46 times during his first year in office, compared with President George W. Bush's 147 such gatherings and 252 for President Clinton in his first twelve months in the White House.[27]

Washington says that this reduction in access to the president demonstrates what has been the reality for many minority journalists with previous administrations. So where is the balance? What more needs to be done to hold the White House accountable?

Our discussion covers a range of concerns, from the representation of African Americans in the media to the impact of the sound bite on the news agenda.

We begin our conversation discussing the media's relationship with Obama during his 2008 run for the White House.

Linn: Initially, in some sectors of the black media there was a real divergence in coverage of the Obama candidacy, compared to that of the mainstream media, the liberal alternative media, and of course the conservative media.

But media across the board treated then–Senator Obama with some curiosity. Who is this guy? Where is he coming from? How and why is his candidacy surging so much?

Then as he started winning more primaries and his candidacy started amassing more potential, from an outside chance to "Wow, maybe this could be historic," he started getting more coverage.

But one of the problems with the American media and the Obama presidency is that the rise of President Obama runs parallel to the continuing decline in the press. We have an increasing degree of shallow and sensationalistic coverage and less and less probative coverage. On the campaign trail, there were numerous examples of a glaring lack of in-depth coverage, and I think that helped him in some ways but further polluted public consciousness insofar as such coverage negatively affected the very deep-seeded and insidious issue of race in America.

Joanne: You touched on the point that the mainstream press covered the Obama candidacy in a different way than the African American media. How so?

Linn: I don't want to parse things so much because among African American media, there was a rah-rah cheering triumphalist type of coverage. "Wow, it's our guy, he can really do this. Amazing!" That reality comes from the lingering effects of institutionalized racism in America.

But in some segments of the African American media, primarily Web-based outlets, such as BlackCommentator .com which evolved, in part, into *Black Agenda Report*, they had raised serious and in-depth questions about Obama; they were concerned about what he would do and about his potential to neuter and cripple the effort to forthrightly address race. While they haven't come out and said since "we told you so" they do deserve some respect for raising the questions in the first place.

By contrast, during the 2008 presidential campaign, the mainstream media were somewhat hamstrung, in that they wanted to be perceived as being fair to Obama, so a lot of things were just glossed over.

For example, the manufactured blowup around the comments of President Obama's then pastor, Jeremiah Wright. What did Wright say? He was established as being wrong, but what did he say? He was criticized for saying, "Goddamn, America." He was saying "God *damn* America," but why was he saying it? Because of the policies and practices of the government.

There is an important backdrop to Wright's comments. He's from Philadelphia and in the 1990s, the state built *nine* new prisons. Philadelphia, the largest city in the State of Pennsylvania, contributes 43 percent of the prisoners in the Pennsylvania prison system. During the same period, just *one* new high school was built in Philadelphia. We all know, if we're honest about it, that lack of education leads to the conveyor belt that ends up in prison. Yet none of this background and context to Wright's comments was put in the mix by either the mainstream media or even the liberal media.

So as a result of this blowup over Wright, Obama makes his big race speech, "A More Perfect Union," in Philadelphia. But where in the city does he deliver that speech? At the Constitution Center, a fabulously beautiful facility, with multimedia examinations of our nation's founding. But this was a facility that was built in Philadelphia without the involvement of minority contractors or minority workers—no blacks or Hispanics.

There were protests over this systemic exclusion of minority workers, a part of the historic exclusion from the construction industry in Philadelphia. None of that background was a part of the coverage of Obama's race speech, not even tangentially. In some ways, if a reporter from outside of Philadelphia wanted to try to look at that angle, they would not find it, because the city's mainstream media excluded it totally.

So things that really animated what Wright was saying were excluded from the conversation and instead, we got this very shallow spin on him being radical.

Here's another example of the lack of probing and investigation into stories relating to then–Senator Obama and the tone which was set for media coverage of the Obama presidency. There was a speech he gave in San Francisco shortly before the Democratic primary in Pennsylvania. While talking about local reaction to the impact of job losses in the state, Obama said it was not surprising that "they cling to guns or religion or antipathy toward people who aren't like them or anti-immigrant sentiment or anti-trade sentiment as a way to explain their frustrations."[28]

A writer who works with liberal media was offended by this and then it became a big thing, a story.

Well, the reality is if you get outside of Philadelphia and further out into Pennsylvania, you really *do* find yourself in the land of God and guns.

I get around Pennsylvania. I not only cover urban areas but I love to hike and I'll admit, I love to shoot guns every now and then. About sixty miles north of Redding there is a prison industry that employs many prison guards. There are approximately five state prisons and two federal prisons all within a thirty-mile area, and people shoot guns out there all the time.

I'm out there sometimes in the afternoon with a good friend who lives in the area and people will come from work, go to this shooting range, fire off a box of bullets, and then say, "Yeah, I'm leaving and I want to go home and take a shower. Then we'll go to the bar tonight."

So again, there was validity in what Obama was saying but there was very little probative examination by the media, and that's what the responsibility is. But when you look at the media, you see a systemic and structural failing in the coverage of issues of race historically.

If you look at the 1968 Kerner Commission report on civil disorder, aside from the one line that says, "our nation is moving towards two societies, one black, one white," chapter 15 is a very thorough and quite brutal examination of the failures of the media.

It says that one of the problems of the media is that they write from a white man's perspective, as if the whole audience is white. And the Kerner Commission literally indicted the media, not for causing the riots in the 1960s, but for its failure to fully do its job in terms of informing the public regarding the brutality in our society. It also indicted the media of fostering false impressions that reinforced the stereotypes which drive racism individually and institutionally.

Joanne: Another, more recent report, by the Pew Research Center's for Excellence in Journalism, published in 2010, examines the issue of race and media, specifically during the first year of the Obama presidency.

The top "news maker" stories that discussed or highlighted race during the twelve months of the report included, unsurprisingly, President Obama, followed by the arrest of Harvard professor Henry Louis Gates, and then reaction to comments made by Senator Harry Reid in the book *Game Change* suggesting that Barack Obama was only elected president because he was "light skinned" and has "no Negro dialect."

Stories of the black experience fall much lower in the pecking order and lean toward the negative. How has the media attempted to change this dialogue since President Obama came into office?

Linn: The coverage of African Americans hasn't changed in the mainstream press.

The African American press in the United States is generally considered to have been founded in New York City in 1827 with the creation of a newspaper called *Freedom's*

Journal. In March of 1827, they issued their first edition and there was an editorial in there.

The editorial said, "We wish to plead our own cause because for so long others, and even our friends, have spoken wrongly against us." There's another line, and I paraphrase "Our vices are always a raid against us while our virtues are ignored."

That observation in 1827 could be an overlay to the coverage of African-Americans today. The negative aspects of the black community, be it crime or poverty, are covered in depth ad nauseam. Coverage is a mile wide but an inch thick; yet reasons for the crime or the poverty are not covered at all.

The Kerner Commission said that part of the problem was the economic inequalities in America. Well, those economic inequities that were recognized in 1968 have been magnified tenfold. And unfortunately, during the Obama presidency, those economic inequalities have grown wildly with the vast shift in the wealth gap caused in part by the collapse of the housing market, and that really doesn't get a lot of coverage.

Let me give you an example. Back in 2008, a then-unknown congresswoman from Minnesota named Michele Bachmann stood up at a House Financial Services Committee meeting and starts railing about an issue that was based on fundamentally flawed facts.

She said that the Community Reinvestment Act, which was an act to eliminate redlining institutional racism in banking particularly as it applies to the granting of mortgages, was the main reason for the collapse of the mortgage market in the United States. According to that deranged view, it was blacks who caused the mortgage problem in America.[29]

Well, two things. Number one: mortgages that were

given out under the Community Reinvestment Act had a lower default rate than the predatory mortgages that were causing a lot of the collapse in the housing market. No one really pinned her on that factual flaw.

Second, when you dig, as one really good alternative newspaper of Minnesota did, into Michele Bachmann's district, the bottom line is that in individual parts of her district, the black population was no more than 4 percent. Most of them were less than 1 percent. Her district led the State of Minnesota in mortgage foreclosures.

That was *white people* defaulting on mortgages for whatever reasons. So here, Michele Bachmann is blaming the housing crisis on black people, when in fact her own district reflected the contrary. Did anybody really dig into any of this? No.

A few weeks after this, on October 17, 2008, and because of similar comments by others essentially agreeing with her take on the Community Reinvestment Act, Michele Bachmann appeared on *Hardball with Chris Matthews* on MSNBC. So I'm watching and thinking, "Oh, Michele Bachmann. Okay, somebody's going to finally kick her rear end."

Joanne: We're going to get some incisive comment.

Linn: Right. If anybody's going to do it, it's going to be Hardball man. So he was asking these softball questions and I'm like, "Okay Chris, when are you going to bang her on this, man?" Comments like these only served to pour more gasoline on the race fire that was burning on the campaign trail because we had the whole Sarah Palin debacle, where the media ignored her racist past.

Bottom line, Chris Matthews didn't ask any good questions. The conversation meandered around and ended up with Bachmann giving another one of these inane statements that "I wish the American media would take a great look at the views of the people in Congress and find out, are they pro-America or anti-America." That became the focus of the interview, and thus the story that came out of it.

So Chris Matthews had an opportunity and an obligation to examine a seriously inflammatory statement that Bachmann made that would not have positioned him into a "I'm going to stand up on behalf of black people" role. No, it would have been an informational role, a journalistic role. It is his and other journalists' responsibility to correct the record, but he didn't do it on this occasion and it is consistently not done by others who hold the microphone.

Joanne: The press is meant to be the "Fourth Estate," an institution not based on political principles but with a duty to hold public officials accountable

You mentioned earlier the situation with President Obama's former pastor, Jeremiah Wright, and we also witnessed a similar scenario with Shirley Sherrod. The former Georgia State director of rural development was forced to resign after the release of an excerpt of a video from a NAACP event in March 2010. The media clip *appeared* to show Shirley Sherrod describing how she racially discriminated against a white farmer. This turned out to be false, a deliberately manipulated representation of her comment.

Have we got to a point where, ever conscious of ratings and grabbing the public's attention with headlines, journalists and hosts are moving into the position of "opinion maker," where the sound bite and not the story is king?

Linn: Well, the short, concise, cogent, and probative response is *yes.*

What you are talking about in terms of the role of the media is what I talk about constantly, from the introduction to news writing class I teach all the way up to the multimedia news program that I codirect. Media in the United States have the constitutional protection of the First Amendment for two reasons and two reasons only.

The first reason is to provide an informational role so we would have an informed civil society to help propel and protect and preserve democracy; so people know who and what their elected officials and wannabe officials are.

The other purpose is that of the watchdog role. Who's going to check the checkers? The United States government is based on checks and balances—Congress checks the president, the president checks Congress, the courts check both of them. But who's going to check all three of those rascals? That was the job that fell to the media. That's a core reason why we have the constitutional protection—freedom of the press—to make media in this country.

Today, too many people seem to have forgotten both of those purposes of the media and have moved away from it as if it doesn't exist; although we as journalists are the first to wrap ourselves up in the protections of the constitution like a bulletproof vest. Today, too much of the media is dominated by TV's talking heads and the shock jocks of radio. Most of these are not journalists.

So who do we have? We have a Chris Matthews, we have a Stephanopoulos, but these people are not grounded as journalists.

Do they do a good job at what they do? Yes, they do. But

my point more so is that the journalists, the boots-on-the-ground people, the people who are doing the actual reporting, are being pushed back to the margins.

We have talking heads who are taking talking points from this one, that one, and the other one, and serious topics worthy of probative attention take on another tone or are lost altogether. There are a lot of structural and institutional issues with the media that are not being addressed.

Now, because say Fox has done so well with polluting its audience base, what did the other media try to do? Emulate Fox but with a slightly less right wing approach and tone, but stylistically, the same.

Joanne: Let's go back to the liberal media's reaction and coverage of then–Senator Obama in the 2008 presidential campaign and the relationship that was born during that time; you want to expand on this . . .

Linn: The liberal media was trying to show just how liberal it is and thus how fair we could be. But in doing so, I think it neutered itself because it did have a responsibility to not only look at Obama as a viable candidate and see what he was saying, but look at everybody else and also themselves.

When we look at these studies that come out year after year after year after year in terms of the levels of diversity or lack thereof in the media, much of it is always focused on the mainstream media. Forty-eight percent of newspapers in America, according to the American Society of News Editors, don't have any minority staff at all. We have newspapers in Native American country, in Oklahoma and places like that, yet no Native Americans on their staff. How does that happen?

It's replicated among Hispanics, African Americans, and other minority groups. But no one takes a look at the liberal media in terms of *its* lack of diversity and the liberal media as represented by the online, Web-based publications. It's even worse than the traditional print-based or broadcast-based media. Notions of inclusiveness and expansiveness of ideas that are meant to shape the coverage are simply not there.

Do liberal media do a better job of looking in-depth at issues involving race and the institutional aspects of racism? In many instances, yes, they do. But there are some very serious problems here that we just do not address. I think that is a detriment to the media and it has been a detriment to really looking at things related to Obama the person and the policies of the Obama administration.

Joanne: A number of questions have been raised about President Obama the person and his response to the media. There was a moment early in his presidency when it felt as though he was everywhere: on the cover of *Essence* with his family, in *Vanity Fair*, in *GQ*, on the *Jay Leno Show*. These were positive presentations of the first black president of the United States.

But, there have been instances where racial comments have been made. For example, in January 2010, quotes from Senator Harry Reid in the book *Game Change* surfaced, in which he said that Obama only became president because he didn't speak with a "Negro dialect."

In terms of how Obama has responded to comments like these, accepting apologies and moving on, what impact have his actions had on the way race and racism is covered by the American press, especially among conservative and mainstream media?

Linn: I think fundamentally that Barack "Barry" Obama has brought a different tone to politics. He wants to bring people together, and from the campaign debates forward, his good manners have made those with a meaner style look small and less intelligent. However, his insistence on being a nice guy has also been destructive and quite baffling, as in his insistence on bipartisanship and making friends with enemies and people who would rather have him chopped up and his body parts given out as souvenirs like they did during lynching.

That said, I don't think it's Obama's job to point out the failings of the media. But because of his reticence to really tackle race, be that tactical or be that the fact that the man just doesn't have any backbone, that is the real issue.

With the arrest of the Harvard professor Henry Louis Gates outside his own home, Obama's first reaction to what the cop did was to say, "That's stupid." And that was right because it *was* stupid. But when he faced criticism for his remarks he backed out, he ran away and then held a beer summit. Well, excuse me. Police brutality is a problem in the United States.

The people who love him on the left—and also those who hate him on the right—criticize or praise him for being an embodiment of King's dream. Well, let's look at the dream piece. When you read the whole speech or listen to it, the "I have a dream" portion comprises two paragraphs in a long presentation. Before you get to "I have a dream," King talked about the American nightmare and in that American nightmare, as he laid out in that speech in August of 1963, he specifically mentioned police brutality as a problem twice. Twice!

It has continued to be a problem, and the situation with

Henry Louis Gates and President Obama's reaction could've started a discussion, by saying not only did the officer abuse his authority because Massachusetts law specifically did not give him the authority or the discretion to do what he did, but it could also have been used to leapfrog into the larger issue of police abuse which is systemic and which also drives the big incarceration figures. The problem with police abuse is not just the fatal shootings, which are horrific, or the beatings, which are bad, but the false arrests.

We have *tens of thousands* of people in jail serving time because of police abuse, the type of police abuse that never gets any kind of recognition. President Obama could've done something with that but he didn't. Furthermore, the person who was abused by a police officer was a personal friend and mentor of his. Now, if you're not going to stand up for your friend, somebody who you know, are you going to stand up for an abstract community? I don't think that's going to happen.

Joanne: You say abstract community, but it's his community. Given his background as a community organizer in Chicago, President Obama is not unaware of these issues. The problems facing African Americans are not abstract to him.

Linn: Yes, he does have an element of responsibility but I have argued since his election that he doesn't have an obligation to address issues of import to African Americans because of his black ancestry. He has a responsibility because he is the President of the United States, and if there's a problem affecting any portion of the United States, it is the responsibility and the duty and the obligation of the president to address that. But let's look at him vis-à-vis this community. Obama grew up in a white household and thus, his orientations are not the same as someone who grew up in the hood.

To be clear, I am not suggesting that there is any virtue of growing up in the hood. I grew up in the hood but when I moved into the neighborhood in Pittsburgh that I grew up in in 1958, it was only 20 percent black. White Americans benefited from the largess from FHA mortgages and government-backed mortgages that enabled them to move out of the cities and into the suburbs for as little as one hundred dollars down; that didn't also happen for black folks.

So, this notion of segregation and racism, we lived it. I lived it, my parents lived it. It is not something from a dim and distant past; it is not something limited to the days of Nat Turner and Harriet Tubman. It's still very much a part of the American experience being lived out today.

To give a further example, a young man gets racially profiled and arrested on use of marijuana. He and his partners—all white—are in a car. One of the guys goes into the mall to buy some weed. Unbeknownst to him, the guy who's selling the weed had been previously arrested and has now agreed to help the cops set up a sting. The police officer monitoring the transaction follows the kid out of the mall. He gets in the car, they look at the bag of weed and they say, "Oh, it's light. It's not a full ounce that we paid for."

So to check it out, everybody passed the bag of weed around to confirm what they felt. When it gets into the one black guy's hands, that's when the police make the arrest. The officer saw who purchased it and watched the bag go around the car. The only person he arrests in the car is the black kid, not the white kid who made the buy.

Now, I know that if he goes to court by himself, he's not

coming home, so I go to court with him; I'm not a lawyer, but I do have a law degree from Yale and have specialized in the law as an investigative reporter for thirty years.

At the hearing, a court official says, "Anybody who's represented by a lawyer come to the front. The rest of you stand in line."

I know the dynamics of courts so I told the kid, "Take that little pin out of your lip, put on a suit, get out of your skateboarding gear, dress up, comb your hair."

When the prosecutor comes out, he's crisp and sharp and he looks down the line and says, "Everybody who's represented by a lawyer, come up to the front."

There are two people in the line with a suit me and another guy way in the back who looked like he'd slept in his suit for three days. I'm black, he's white. The prosecutor walks past me like I'm not even there. He goes to the back and says, "Sir, I said that anybody who is represented by a lawyer, please come to the front. Are you a lawyer?" The guy says, "No, I'm not a lawyer. I'm here for drunk driving."

Now, the prosecutor assumed that the other guy in the line with a suit on who was white had to be a lawyer because everybody else had on T-shirts, jeans, and other stuff. But from his viewpoint, from his eyesight, I couldn't have been in that community of lawyers. However, the other guy with the suit on may have been that. That's the kind of subtle piece in terms of everyday institutional racism that persists in this country to this day.

So we have these sorts of issues and this gets all the way back, in a very circular way, to Obama.

Joanne: The example you give highlights, perhaps, the differences in the upbringing of President Obama and the real world experiences of many African Americans.

Linn: I don't think that his background gives him these kinds of insights. Look at his experience; he's always wanted to try to find a way to fit in because where he lived and his lifestyle, he was always the outsider, be it Indonesia, Hawaii, or Kansas, or the Eastern elite schools where he studied. So he wants to make friends and he wants to play down the issue of race because it's been so contentious.

Joanne: President Obama's personal experiences aside, do you agree that the White House communications team and the Obama presidency has circumnavigated the traditional pathways of accountability via the media with an increased use of online tools? For example, ABC News White House correspondent Ann Compton says that access has been narrowed to "an unprecedented extent."

Linn: I would argue differently, and not just in stark terms, because I think one of the quintessential failings of the Obama administration is that it has failed to get its story out there, be it in social media, mainstream media, liberal media, or be it in their own press passing out flyers in front of the White House. There have been a lot of successes during this administration to date, including some successes specific to black people, but who knows about them?

Back in 2010, I received a list from a professor who specializes in the office of the president, detailing the accomplishments of the Obama administration to date. It went on for seven single-spaced pages. As I made my way through the document, I kept saying "My goodness, why isn't any of this known in the media?" What is wrong with the White House in terms of being able to tell its story? They have done an abysmal job.

Social media were used adroitly during Obama's 2008 presidential campaign. That created a base for Obama, but what did he do when he got in? His team turned over the list of names to the Democratic National Convention and walked away from it.

So on the health care debate, do you think they sent tweets out to all of these people on the list? Or reached out via Facebook? That could've helped turn the tide for him. Despite what many say, I believe that they have not done a good job in exploiting media, be it social media or be it the more traditional media. I think that's one of the serious failings of the Obama presidency.

Joanne: So even though some in the mainstream media complain of being "frozen out" of the Obama administration, especially during the days of the former White House press secretary, Robert Gibbs, social media haven't been used effectively to reach the public directly?

Linn: Exactly. That aside though, I can't give credence to the argument from the mainstream media about being frozen out. For decades the African American media, the Native American media, the Hispanic media have been frozen out of White House press conferences. Now who stood up in the mainstream media and said, "Wait, why are there no black reporters or correspondents here?" They did none of this.

I remember doing an interview with the Washington

correspondent for the National Newspaper Publishers Association, which is the trade organization for 205 black newspapers around the country. This was during the Bush presidency in 2003. The correspondent was bemoaning the fact that after two years, she still hadn't gotten her White House credentials, in spite of being from a bona fide certified news organization. Yet credentials were given to conservative columnist Jeff Gannon, even though at the time, his journalistic experience was limited and there were reports of him working as a male escort.

So because some inside-the-beltway folks don't like the lack of access that they're getting now, too bad.

As a reporter, I would like to have my calls returned. But I've been in this business from the black media side and I've worked for mainstream media. I worked for the *Philadelphia Daily News* for ten years. When I worked there, my calls came back quickly. When I'm doing a story for one of the alternative newspapers, my calls get returned quickly. When I'm with the black media, I've got to jump up and down to get people to give me a call back.

Joanne: In recent months we've seen the White House conduct Facebook town halls, a weekly address that goes out online, daily e-mail alerts and various videos that are posted on YouTube. I know you said that the Obama administration hasn't made the best use of the lists and the contacts made during the 2008 campaign, but by working intensely with electronic communications, getting questions directly from we, the people, so to speak—how effective has this strategy been?

Linn: It has been effective in that it has been utilized, but the utilization hasn't effectively helped shape a message that generates support and thus wins the war. Is it nice that President Obama has these town hall meetings online? Sure it is. But it's just a recognition of the evolution of media and the pace at which things are changing.

Just making use of social media doesn't mean that you're winning the war; you win a few battles with it.

"We had a million people take part in the town hall," but what did those million people do? Well, they went back to tweeting, Facebooking, and Four Squaring. "Yeah, where are we going to be for beer? Oh, let's go here." "Did you take part in Obama's presidency?" "Yes, I did. But who cares about that?" "Yeah, you're right. I'll meet you at seven."

By contrast, the conservative media, is active in getting their message out there. "Obama health care, reparations for black people—we can't have that." Obama specifically said that he does not favor reparations for black folks and that turned off the 10 percent in the black community who want that. He's lost their vote forever because he's turned his back on reparations.

But conservatives turned the health care conversation into a hysterical claim about reparations for blacks. And imagine this. You have to get sick to get some recompense for the institutional racism that made you sick. Geez, yeah, you could keep that $1.35.

Joanne: And this comes back to who controls the news agenda. But what about the African American media? You touched on it a little bit in terms of what it's like trying to get a call returned from the White House or trying to get your questions answered. Quite often it's the black press where you'll find the most analysis, yet African American reporters probably have the least amount of access. We can complain about it, but what responsibility do black reporters have to advocate for the information that we need to be able to serve our community better?

Linn: Well, two things. One, Obama has done something that no other U.S. president has done consistently before him. Every now and then he does call black reporters for mainstream media as well as some from the black press.

People in black media—at the publisher level, editor level, and reporter level—are just as conflicted about how to deal with the Obama presidency as are folks in the rest of the black community.

We're not a monolithic community. There are conservatives, liberals, and others. But the black press has been conflicted because they're saying, "Listen, Obama's our guy," and we have this collective pride in him being there and that's natural and understandable given the nature and context and the ongoing daily reality of race in this country. If we criticize Obama, does that give more ammunition to the critics on the right who've been waging a withering war against him? Black reporters sometimes don't quite know which way to go.

But you're starting to see a ramping up of criticism of Obama in the black press too, not just a castigating criticism like you see from the conservative side. But real questions are being asked about areas we've been shortchanged on during Obama's presidency so far, including jobs, minority contracting, and so on.

According to the Kirwan Institute on race studies at Ohio

State University, under the stimulus funding, black businesses have secured 3.5 percent of all the contracts. So the first response of the more enlightened conservative is, "Well, there's no black business in America." Well, 7.1 percent of all the businesses in America are owned by blacks, yet they've received just 3.5 percent of stimulus-funded contracts. And when black businesses are awarded stimulus contracts, they tend to be of low dollar value.[30]

These are the kinds of inequities that a president of the United States needs to address but these issues have yet to be addressed.

Joanne: More and more, people live their lives online; communicating, catching news stories, and so on. In recent times, we've seen the *Huffington Post* integrate *Black Voices* into their site, and *The Griot* and *The Root*, which is owned by the *Washington Post*.

Do you see that even in a small way, and especially with online media, that the outlets and the opportunities for stories of interest to African Americans beyond stories about incarceration rates and racism—are being made available? Are we witnessing more diversity in the coverage of the African American experience?

Linn: Yes. That widening of venues for telling the story has increased during the Obama administration but had John McCain gotten in, it would've done the same thing because what we're really talking about is just the evolution of the media and particularly the evolution of Internet-based media.

These stories that you're talking about beyond the traditional "here's the latest study confirming what you already knew about high incarceration rates," that takes place online, yes. The fact that the *Washington Post* would do various online efforts is a recognition that online is where things are going.

So I don't think the Obama presidency has had some primacy in the proliferation of these online venues, and particularly those directed toward black audiences, be they black owned and controlled or black focused but white controlled. But it's just something that would've happened anyway with or without him.

Joanne: The stories are one thing, the employment of journalists of color is something else. Even though we're seeing an expansion in online media, what's the true story of diversity within newsrooms?

Linn: No improvements. In fact, there is a very decided and alarmingly rapid reverse in the trend. Blacks are being pushed *out* of newsrooms. There's the push because they get fed up with what they don't get in terms of promotional opportunities first off. Then there are the economic contractions in the industry.

A couple of years ago, the *Philadelphia Inquirer*, because of money issues, had to reduce its staff tremendously. In the process, what happened? Most of the minorities were washed out the door. Just recently, the top African American editor—we're talking at the managing editor level—was let go. And the *Philadelphia Inquirer* now has a metropolitan city reporting staff that has literally a handful of reporters of color and you could still probably have four or five fingers left of blacks.

So I don't see a healthy trend going forward, even as we become a much, much more multiracial, multicultural society.

Joanne: How is the black agenda and issues important to African Americans going to be a part of the news cycle in future elections if newsrooms are light on diverse voices and perspectives?

Linn: The short answer for me is just do what you're supposed to do and that's to be thorough in the coverage and be mindful of the role of dissemination of information as well as being a watchdog.

In 2008 the media was highly focused on historic qualities of Obama's run for the White House. Well, there was another historic candidacy; there was the historic candidacy of the Green Party where its presidential candidate was a woman named Cynthia McKinney and the vice-presidential candidate was Rosa Clemente, the first Hispanic to ever run in that position. Rosa Clemente was a journalist and there was zero coverage of this. You put Cynthia McKinney into LexisNexis and you get about 145 articles. Put in Sarah Palin and the machine stops up because it's more than three thousand over any two-week period in the fall of 2008.

Yes, we still have a way to go.

SIX

It Matters What Needs to Be Done

Politics and Green Activism with Van Jones

By listening to a cross section of some of the fifty thousand tapes in the Pacifica Radio Archives spanning over sixty years, it is clear that history repeats itself. Issues are duplicated. The themes of obligation, service, and a desire to change the world for good are the common threads that duck and weave through the narratives of activists, campaigners, and agents for social change immortalized on tape in the archives' cold climate-controlled vault.

As a radio journalist, I deal in the currency of voice, what is being said openly along with the depth of emotion sometimes hidden in a turn of phrase, a barely audible sigh, a quickened tone, or a subtle inflection.

Listening to recordings that span the heart of the black freedom movement over the years, I noticed how the tone changed in the delivery of each message and the evolution of the platforms activists used to be heard. At a critical point, the voices would no longer be silent or go unheard; relentless determination was being marshaled against injustice; the measured tones of Rosa Parks recalling why she decided to sit in the front of a segregated bus; James Baldwin's boiling anger as he recounted the deaths of four little girls as a result of the terrorist attacks against Birmingham's Sixteenth Street Church. Taking in the words of Fannie Lou Hamer, you feel the weight of every blow she received as she relives the trauma of being attacked while trying to register to vote. And in 1968, Stokely Carmichael and H. Rap Brown verbally and emotionally elevated a community of Black Panthers at a Free Huey rally in Oakland, California.

Scroll forward to the present day. The platform for many of today's activists consists of more than just a megaphone, rallies, pamphlets, and word of mouth. Electronic communications are transforming the ways in which activists conduct outreach, advocacy, fundraising, campaigns, and movement building. Activists can be at home and still get their message across. Some find their way into public office at the local and state levels, others take the opportunity to become a part of the government machinery in an attempt to exert change from within.

Crossing over from the traditional activist realm of the street and the courtroom isn't an easy one to navigate. How do you maintain your street cred while speaking the language of those who work in the corridors of power? Having listened to so many activists express themselves during the civil rights and black power years via audio, I wasn't altogether sure this could be done without some kind of compromise or personal cost.

On entering the office of Van Jones, I was struck by his energy: at once disciplined, driven, and determined, but also responsive and charming. As an activist who fought in the trenches against police brutality in Oakland, California, and who took his "Green Jobs, Not Jail" message all the way to the White House, it's no surprise when Van Jones says of his guiding ethic: It matters what needs to be done.

Listening to this within the context of our conversation about President Obama and the lives of African Americans, I thought of the campaign slogan of the first African American woman to run for the White House in 1972, Shirley Chisholm: Unbought and Unbossed. In many ways this also applies to Van Jones.

Van Jones's progressive career has spanned from highs and lows; from applause over his appointment as the Obama administration's Green Jobs Adviser to jeers and a public teardown at the hands of the right-wing press over his activist past, which ultimately led to his resignation. His mission has since evolved with the "American Dream Movement." Its mission? To restore the nation with jobs, education, dignity, and real hope for the future.

Van Jones is marching forward, doing what needs to be done for his country, community, and family. The office surroundings have changed, but the goal remains the same.

A master multitasker, during our conversation Van Jones didn't just talk, he texted, e-mailed, and researched facts on his computer without missing a beat.

Jones strikes me as a leader who is every inch the hybrid, a product of the many lives he has lived and experiences he has embraced and endured. A street-savy activist whose credibility, refined demeanor, quick wit and sharp intellect brings together seemingly different worlds—those of civil rights and a sustainable green future.

We began our conversation peeking into Van Jones's life in activism and how he became politically engaged at an early age.

Van: I was born in 1968 and I really don't remember not being politically interested, even in kindergarten and first grade. We had these things called Weekly Readers where they would have little stories for us to read. Anything that was about the Kennedy brothers or Dr. King, I would cut with my little round scissors and take it home and stick it up on my little bulletin board. Other kids had superheroes or athletes on their wall. I had Bobby Kennedy and Dr. King. When I got a little older, I changed all my *Star Wars* figures' names to political people; JFK was Han Solo.

One of my earliest memories is of seeing an African American woman on television giving a speech. She talked funny. I remember asking my uncle Chester, "Why does she talk funny?" And he said, "She has a lisp." It was Shirley Chisholm at the 1972 Democratic Convention. I wasn't even four years old. Most kids that age were probably doing something other than watching televised coverage of the Democratic Convention with their uncle. Some people started piano or ballet when they were young; for me it was politics.

Joanne: You've talked publicly about your experiences as a student at Yale; how you would see young, privileged white students doing drugs. They'd be sent to rehab a few blocks down the street, but it was a very different story for African Americans within the community.

You've done a lot of work looking at police brutality over the years. How do you feel that relationship between African Americans and the police, in particular, has changed since your early activist days?

Van: During the 1990s, African Americans were the number one threat in the social imagination of many Americans. In the 2000s, the Muslim, Arab, and Middle Easterner has taken on that role as public villain. And in some ways, at least in terms of the public conversation, there's been a shift.

However, the incarceration rates and those kinds of things are still shockingly high for African Americans. So, we're in this interesting period where kids say that there's racialized public fear that requires a state response, a government response, a police response.

The immigrant at the southern border, the Arab possibly coming to do harm through our airlines, and the African American kid on the street, all represent different aspects of the relationship between police power and disadvantaged people.

Most African American communities are not well-served by their police forces. It's a combination of abuse and neglect that communities suffer with.

Joanne: Addressing issues of racialized policing is directly related to other work you've done around unjust incarceration practices.

Van: And I couldn't do that work very long. I burned out after probably five or six years. My journey toward trying to find more comprehensive solutions really came out of my exhaustion with trying to reform the incarceration industry.

The pursuit of profit corrupts a big chunk of the criminal justice system. One disturbing result is the emergence of private for-profit prisons. Even publicly owned prisons have no incentive to reform anybody because if you're a prison warden and you send somebody home and they come back in a year with four more people, your budget gets bigger and you don't lose your job.

These perverse incentives within the criminal justice system grow at the expense of poor communities; at the expense of any sense of a just society. Underneath that is the deepening problem of joblessness and despair in communities that have led to an increase in policing, an increase in incarceration, an increase in prison building instead of an increase in investing in our communities and addressing why we continue to permit the wealthy to get wealthier while the poor get poorer.

Seeing the enormity of the problem, I began to push for jobs and economic development as a possible solution. I had the slogan "Green Jobs, Not Jails" starting in the early 2000s because I felt there was some link between the idea of a throwaway people and a throwaway planet. For me, the idea of *disposability* does an awful lot of damage. If we could resist both and say, "God didn't make any junk," and people in communities and all the species are precious, then that might be a door to better politics. Not just in terms of externally having more success, but internally having more coherence, and more joy, and more beauty.

There are deeper problems still, some of which have to do with, for lack of a better term, *the malfeasance of the finance capital*—predatory banks and financial practices in the United States deepening the problems for people and whole communities. Add to that the entrenched practices of the military-petroleum-complex—the Pentagon and profit-driven corporations—that spends staggering amounts to get oil, coal, and natural gas out of the ground and into the marketplace.

But additional billions and trillions in resources are required from the Pentagon to release and protect all the oil supply routes involved. If we were to redeploy a piece of all the intellectual capital and subsidies now going to big corporations and direct that piece toward clean and green solutions, we would be contributing to being more energy secure and be creating better jobs for more people. There are so many ways to begin. One is to "Green the Ghetto," as urban revitalization strategist Majora Carter is famous for saying back in 2006.

I went from battling the incarceration industry to battling the military-petroleum-complex. The arena is bigger, there are more allies, including environmentalists, clean-tech investors, students, and all kinds of folks who would like to see us have a greener, cleaner America.

Joanne: Earlier you talked about not being able to stay in that mind-set of battling in terms of bringing down the incarceration rate for black men and women. When we look back at the likes of Fannie Lou Hamer and Rosa Parks and even further back to Harriet Tubman and Frederick Douglass, would you say being an activist can be a lonely existence?

Van: Anything you do by yourself can be hard. It really depends on the personality. I think I tend to build decent teams, so I've always had lots of company in the work. But, it can still be very difficult.

Most people aren't activists, not because they don't care about the world but because they aren't convinced that the payoff makes sense; that what you have to put out personally to make a very small change is quite a lot, and what you get back, personally, is probably maybe an award or an organizational dinner in your honor every few years from the non-profit community.

So, a particular mind-set is required. You have to believe it's worth it to go through all that you have to go through in order to make change. But it's a tough path to walk; mounting direct attacks against well-fortified positions from places of less power is often a formula for burnout.

For most of my twenties, I was going direct. There's the enemy. There's the problem. There's the injustice. I worked in a very linear way, but with no allies, no money, no real hope of victory, just doing it because it was the right thing to do.

Battles were won that way, but at a tremendous personal cost in terms of health and well-being. I had a big victory in 1997. I had a big victory in 2003. But, in five years, it wasn't like I was sitting around drinking lattes. We were out there every day protesting, organizing, calling press conferences, going to conferences.

It's a very demanding lifestyle. But for me, I wasn't going to give up on the prospect of justice, but I wasn't going to continue to do things that I could see after a couple of cycles, we could do that for one thousand years and still have a whole bunch of people in prison.

Joanne: And now there are other considerations stemming from the ongoing economic crisis and increasing poverty.

Van: As I look out, it really looks like it's going to be hard to fix any of the other issues in America as long as the banks continue to be permitted to act the way they do. That's really the fundamental problem in American politics as far as I'm concerned, and you can't jump start the green revolution with credit frozen. You can't do anything.

You can't stabilize communities and prevent people from being fed into the incarceration industry if you can't get business loans, if you can't get student loans, if you can't keep a person from losing their house or apartment and becoming homeless.

Casino banksters took Americans' money and ran. They're still doing it.

Joanne: What can be done to turn things around?

Van: Organizations like the American Federation of Labor and Congress of Industrial Organizations (AFL-CIO), the National Association for the Advancement of Colored People, and others are starting to take a different crack at this and there are some good ideas. There's going to be something called "financial regulatory reform" which will aim to make Wall Street pay back America. That's really the right way to think about it. There should be a whole series of things, not just to prevent banksters from getting away with predatory practices, but also to make them partners in rebuilding America.

In addition to that, we need a green agenda, a small-business agenda, a student's agenda, a community agency; a whole bunch of agendas working together. We need a comprehensive view with clear underlying values.

What are the underlying values here? One is that we don't like the way rich people influence policies in their own favor; we don't like people playing with our money in a way that's not fair to us. But you're not going to win a fight in the United States with that.

Our financial institutions, especially when they're alive only because of taxpayer money, should be our partners but that's not how they're acting. They're acting like pimps.

We need to cohere serious opposition to abuse by our financial institutions and secure real investment and opportunity so we can jump start the green revolution and everything else that we need to do in the country.

Joanne: Much of what you have outlined as issues will impact on our youth and the United States they will inherit. As part of this project, we recorded a panel with three eighteen to twenty-five-year-olds, all politically active in the Los Angeles area. They are concerned that President Obama won't help their future, nor that anything will change for them as young people of color. How do you see youth being instrumental in pushing through what people like you have started?

Van: Young people are right to think that nothing's going to change just because we have a black president. There are black presidents all over Africa and the Caribbean. Blackness is almost wholly irrelevant to having a good, decent, courageous and intelligent president such as we have. What *might* make a difference is if the rest of us acted in ways that are good, and decent, and intelligent, and acted in concert *with* him.

There are three forces driving positive change in the United States right now. The first is technology; the information technology that's continuing to develop smarter and better ways for people to find each other and find good ideas.

Second is the green revolution and all of the technological possibilities that it creates with regard to clean energy and clean technology.

The third force is made up of the millennials—the generation of eighteen to twenty-five-year-olds—who are steeped in digital technology, media and communications, and who are bearing the brunt of the economic downturn. There are more of them and as a group they are more diverse than the boomers. Politically more progressive, they will be heard from and they will rewrite a lot of the more foolish things that we have; the idea that the government has some interest in moderating which gender you marry. That's fairly foolish and a big waste of time. So, the millennials will just take that off the books at some point. There's an expiration date on a lot of the really stupid things because they just won't put up with it.

Joanne: What's spurring the millennials to continue the work of civil rights activism? Recent generations have been reluctant to act, almost embracing a "Whatever, I don't care" attitude.

Van: Every generation has its own identity, and this one is a much more hands-on, problem-solving generation. They're much less caught up in a lot of the identity nonsense from even well-intentioned people in all the generations. The millenials fueled the Obama phenomenon and have a strong service ethic.

These young people connect more on the basis of subcultures than on the basis of racial groups. So, if you like hip-hop, then you're connecting with people in that sphere. If you like skateboarding, you're in another sphere. If you like particular video games, then you're in with those folks. There's less of the leaning on the primacy of racial categories. I think this trend is really healthy, quite welcome, and long overdue. It makes for more dynamic politics because as long as everybody stays in their own little stand, big folks win. Little folks win when we get a little bit unpredictable, as when white women vote for a black man in massive numbers. That shook up the Democratic Party and, ultimately, shook up American politics. Hillary Clinton couldn't just say, "Well, I'm a white woman, so all the white women are going to vote for me." That's not what happened.

Joanne: And likewise with Barack Obama and black voters.

Van: It's the age of the hybrid: hybrid cars, hybrid kids. I have two hybrid kids and hybrid politics. So, for me, mixing up civil rights and the green agenda is interesting—it brings together groups and arguments, and resources, and contacts in innovative ways.

For example, part of what we've seen from the Heritage Foundation and others, is that they've thrown millions of dollars trying to *stop* the green jobs movement. They're not spending a lot of time and energy at the same level and the same ferocity, trying to stop other, more predictable things, coming out of our communities.

Joanne: But what benefit is there to anyone in trying to stop the green revolution?

Van: I think they're trying to stop it because it's a viable alternative worldview and set of policies that threatens the petroleum industry. I also think that the way that they approach this is influenced by the fact that I'm African American, but they would come at it anyway.

If there was a Latina lesbian who was able to get the

Democratic Party into the White House, everybody would just start posing this stuff differently. They would come after her too. The idea that we could actually leave the coal and the oil in the ground and power America on clean energy, and have a different set of businesses flourish, just doesn't make the oil industry's CEOs happy.

Joanne: Somebody's going to lose money.

Van: Exactly, or, "I got to work harder to make the same amount of money." That's also losing money.

Joanne: You've somehow managed to create this hybrid of civil rights activism and green initiatives. But, is it palatable on the street when you go into black and brown communities? Are they saying, "Van, have you lost your mind? What am I meant to do with a solar panel when I can't feed my children?" What are people on the street actually saying to you?

Van: Well, it depends. People on the street ask me that question a lot. I never quite know what to do with it. Probably, to the extent that regular folks hear what I'm saying, they hear me saying *green* very softly and *jobs* very loudly. So, green jobs, purple jobs, plaid jobs.

Joanne: Jobs. Work.

Van: Yes. So, probably for people who are materially desperate, that's their main access point. And then, they want to know, is there a job in all this? It's a very long arc from policy to economic opportunity to job creation.

That said, in some ways, I win these arguments by default. When we shake up the energy business and create space for new innovation, new products, new technologies, new entrepreneurs, new employment opportunities, new employment pathways, we will also be creating many new career pathways.

At the end of the day, we're talking about a lot of money. And there's no other play in the U.S. economy that even comes close in terms of benefits. We're talking about redoing the transportation fleet. We're talking about redoing the grid. We're talking about tapping the wind and solar energy we have *here*; letting America do for itself what we have always relied on other countries to do for us in terms of empowering the country going forward. We'll be more energy independent. We'll be more secure.

That's a lot. I don't want to overclaim for it, but what's the rival opportunity? There is none. And so, you're talking about manufacturing. . . .

Joanne: That's gone.

Van: Exactly, it's gone. So, we had to get very aggressive renewable energy goals here, so there was certainty of demand. You would actually have an incentive to build the wind turbines here because they're just too big to build in Asia, transport across the ocean, and then drive across the country.

So, if you had certainty of demand, if you had the right policy environment, you could actually get Indiana, Michigan, and Ohio going from a rust belt to a green belt and have those blue-collar workers becoming green-collar workers. People then wouldn't say, "What are you talking about?"

They'd say, "How can we start?" And then, you're in a different world. You've got to deal with the financial capital being frozen and the wrong policy environment first. But, then you get very quickly from "what are you talking about" to "how can I be a part of it."

Joanne: Your work has grown through the fact that President Obama understood and supported what you are trying to do. He saw the connection between jobs and helping us to have a green and glorious planet. Do you feel that African Americans have somehow progressed, that things have somehow changed, that there is a difference, that things are easier, worse, somewhere in between, now that there's an African American president?

Van: I think that Obama's victory inspires the world. In that regard, I think it should take the ceiling off of individuals' expectations for their own lives. President Obama is not a rich man's child; his father was an immigrant. So, if your father or mother was an immigrant, if you had a ceiling on your expectations in this country, it should come off.

He's obviously African American, so if you're African American and you had a ceiling on your expectations about your life, it should come off.

He's also of mixed race, so if you're feeling like you don't fit in, you're a mongrel, you're a mutt, and that there's a limit on what you can do, then that ceiling should come off.

I think that at a subjective level for any individual, there should be a renewed sense of confidence and determination not to let the world tell you what you can do and what you can't do.

At an objective level, in terms of are people going to be more or less racist toward you, or more or less accepting, or more or less embracing of your immigrant background, I think that's a pretty dubious proposition because we've always had the "exceptional Negro" whether you go back to Frederick Douglass, or DuBois, or in popular culture today, Michael Jordan, Michael Jackson, Oprah Winfrey, Colin Powell.

America has always been able to make room for the truly exceptionally gifted African American without necessarily dislodging any of her skepticism and suspicion about the rest of us.

And so, I think that the effect probably will be most profound within the individuals who look to Obama for inspiration. I would say, in that regard, Barack Obama's biggest legacy will not be as president, but as *precedent*. That's really going to be his biggest contribution. He will do an awful lot as president, but as you can see in this town, Washington, DC, if you try to do an awful lot, you suffer an awful lot and it's just very, very difficult. So, he may have come in with a to-do list of a hundred goals, he may only get to the first three before his eight years are up. But, if God were to call him home today, one hundred years from now, people would still be inspired by his story and he would still be creating good in the world because of the precedent that he set.

Joanne: His election and the whole campaign brought people out in droves and engaged people in politics in a way not previously seen. Do you feel that there's enough momentum behind Obama for people to continue to organize and take an interest in activism and politics through his tenure?

Van: No. There were some singular convergences in American life in 2008. Mainly real frustration with George Bush as well as real hope in Obama, along with a real desire to see more integrity and intelligence in the White House that created that huge explosion.

Right now, I would say the hope bubble has collapsed and that the last time you saw people really take to the streets and be really loud and proud was the inauguration. After the inauguration, people just disappeared, and then out came the Tea Party movement as a backlash.

The forces for hope and change, the movement for hope and change, which really preceded Obama's White House run, is struggling to reignite itself. This movement for hope and change really goes back two hundred years, but in its most recent form, it probably really started in 2003 when Bush launched his illegal invasion against the people of Iraq, and people in their millions came out to march, and protest, and to work against it.

That year the *New York Times* called us "the second super power"[31] and then in 2004, we came within one hundred thousand votes in Ohio of getting rid of Bush not just because of enthusiasm for the candidate, but mainly enthusiasm for change and for a new direction for the country.

In 2005, the Katrina catastrophe really sealed the fate of the Republican Party and left a permanent mark on the Bush presidency such that in the 2006 midterm election, the Democrats were able to break the back of one-party authoritarian rule in the United States.

Now note, we did all that without Barack Obama, right? Barack Obama at that point had given an inspirational speech in 2004 at the Democratic National Convention and was a source of some hope and potential in the country, but he wasn't the leader of anything at that point and yet, we achieved an incredible prodemocracy force in the United States, which overpowered the Republicans.

It achieved an incredible victory in 2006 that then opened the door for somebody like Obama to say, "Look. The people are moving." You don't have to have the Clinton machine and the Clinton brand, or the McCain machine and the McCain brand to lead this country because people were already taking leadership.

And so, we have this wonderful merger of man and movement where a potential world-class leader like Obama could step forward and be supported by the people and inspire them.

But, remember, the people inspired him first and that's what we forget. The people inspired him and that's why he had the courage to run. The combination created this very beautiful process that enabled Obama to rise beyond the Clintons and McCain.

Obama, as candidate for the White House, represented not just a political force but a cultural and a spiritual force. He's so inspiring, and an inspired spirit. There was a spiritual revival happening around him. Also, culturally, there was this idea that America could *look* different. It could *be* different. It could overcome some of its more bitter ethics of her legacy.

Joanne: He was that ultimate hybrid.

Van: Exactly. And so, you had a number of convergences that were all happening at the same time and he was able to stand in and represent all of it. He went from being a movement leader and cultural icon that inspired a spiritual revival, to becoming head of state.

A head of state can't run a mass movement or a spiritual revival. The head of state has to run the government and it's not a unitary government. You've got three branches of the government.

So, now we're seeing the spirit collapse. Well, what is that? That's the hope. And then, when the hope collapses, it makes the other part, the change, harder to do. We also have this new force, this new backlash that is gaining in competence and sophistication, and these are difficult days.

Thinking about this only from the point of view of having a black president is very limited in its value. What we're now faced with is one of the most difficult problems in the history of world politics: how does a country whose hope was assassinated with Dr. Martin Luther King Jr. and Bobby Kennedy in 1968 go forty years in the desert with an occasional blip from Jesse Jackson in the 1980s and Bill Clinton in the 1990s (but without ever renewing the sense of national possibility and purpose that we had in the 1960s) and arrive on the doorstep of a new era in November 2008?

The potential for catastrophe is enormous if the Obama *movement* becomes an Obama *moment* that doesn't mark a new direction for the country, but in fact, just marks a temporary reaction on the part of a very fragile coalition to a very particular set of events based mainly on George Bush's failures. My job is to try to help prevent that outcome. This is a job for every prodemocracy activist in the country of whatever color. Those are my commitments going forward.

Joanne: Have Obama's wings been clipped since becoming one of the most politically influential people in the world?

Van: I don't think his wings have been clipped. I think the movement clipped its own wings. I'm holding up a pair of scissors. Which scissor is more important? Which of these is more important than the other?

Joanne: Neither one.

Van: They don't work. You've got to have both pieces. And so, President Obama can't get anything done by himself. His movement, essentially, packed up and went home after the inauguration, and now people are disappointed in the president. People should be disappointed in themselves because it's not his job to run a movement. It's his job to be head of state. That's what we elected him to do.

So, when does it work? It works when you have the right person and the right movement. We inspired Obama first. If there's an inspiration gap or a hope gap, a change gap, that's on *us* to fill.

I remember being in the White House and thinking, "Where did everybody go?" All we're doing is getting criticized up the wazoo by the bloggers. Meanwhile, the opposition is organized, and sending the Orks over the mountain screaming and yelling at us. This is not going to work, folks. There are only a thousand people working in the White House. Fifty-five million people voted him into office.

You tell me, if something's not working, who's responsible at the end of the day, if you're talking about change? If you're talking about just managing the status quo then, fine, you can blame Obama for anything. If you're talking about moving a change agenda forward, he said, "Yes, we can." He didn't say, "Yes, I can." He meant, "Yes, *we*," this movement. And that's really what has to come back.

Joanne: Let's talk about your time within the Obama administration. I asked you about whether you thought that President Obama's effectiveness has been clipped in some way being in the White House, you said no.

But, you have experienced being an activist, being a voice, and being someone trying to effect change from inside the government framework and outside of it. What was your experience working within?

Van: You know, I was very ambivalent about going as I think anybody would be who is a committed activist. Honored to be asked and felt like it was important to answer the call to service. I learned a ton and have way more respect than I have ever had for those who serve in those positions every day; it's tough, tough, tough. Not thankless, but the thanks and the thanklessness run neck and neck most days.

My view about it is that we need to get people everywhere. Change is going to be top down, bottom up, and inside out. It's going to be from big places like the White House, it's going to be from ordinary communities all across the country. It's going to come from inside of people who are out in the world working as agents for change.

And probably the biggest change is that inside-out part, where people take responsibility in their own ways and don't get into history books, but there's a change of consciousness. Just look at the millennials and how they look at the world versus how maybe their grandparents do. That's not a law, or a bill, or a candidate, but real change.

We waste a lot of time on a lot of false distinctions just arguing about which blade of the scissors is the most important. You're not going to get anything done in the United States without having good people in elective office, good people on the streets and on the blogs, walking the halls of Congress and demanding some meetings with somebody besides the intern.

Joanne: Obviously, you're not in that position now, but did you feel that there was more work that you could have done within the administration than trying to do it from the outside?

Van: If I had stayed in the administration, I would've done a bunch of cool stuff. I was doing cool stuff when I was there.

Wherever you are, you can conserve. I'm ambidextrous enough that I have a lot of background. I've been a boss and built stuff, so you can stick me in a place like the White House and I'll perform very well. You could also stick me in a public housing project, or a public school, or a tough neighborhood and I'll do really well there as well because I'm just committed to change. So, wherever I am, whatever assignment you give me, I'm going to try to do it world class.

I think people should experiment with what they like to do. But, it doesn't really matter what you like to do. It matters what needs to be done.

If your country needs you, if your community needs you, you do what needs to be done. Moms don't like doing what they have to do sometimes, but they do it. Dads don't like doing what they must do sometimes, but they do it. I just feel like that's more how I look at this question around inside versus outside.

Joanne: Where do you see the future of black leadership against the backdrop of the Obama presidency?

Van: President Obama has done a remarkable job of getting talented people in his administration—people of every color in the Skittles bag. I think he will continue to do that. I don't think that this president has to do more for African American leadership than Bill Clinton did. But, he's the leader of the Democratic Party. He got a similar percentage of black votes that Bill Clinton got. And so, from a purely political point of view, that's just not his job. He's not a black leader. He's the president of the United States of America.

Joanne: And I guess that's the question. People see him as a black leader.

Van: And I'm sure he would just find that to be kind of remarkable because he was never a race politician.

Joanne: He was never a race politician and he didn't run on a race ticket, but isn't a lot of it down to how people also perceive you?

Van: Well, sure. But, I'm just saying, he was never a race politician. First of all, he ran against Bobby Rush in Chicago. He got beat up bad because people didn't think he was "black enough." He cares about justice, he cares about black people, and he's obviously from a mixed background. But, he certainly has a home in a lot of places and an identity rooted in the black community.

I find a lot of stuff ridiculous; there are functions in politics. It's the NAACP's job to deal with the question of black leadership. It's the Urban League's job. It's Al Sharpton's job. There are functions in politics. It's not the job of the president of the United States.

And so, it's a strange thing. It's like we're kind of outside of history, and outside of civics, and outside of the political system when we start trying to figure out how to have the president do all these jobs and it's not his job to lead a mass movement. It's not his job to fix black America. It's not his job to inspire people every day. He's the head of state.

People act like Barack Obama is going to save America. Good people in America are going to wind up saving Barack Obama, much more likely. And so, we need to get on with it. The president wasn't joking when he said, "This is the beginning, not the end" and that "I can't do this by myself." I think people thought that was just cute campaign rhetoric, but it expresses his understanding about how we're going to change the country.

So, he's doing his role. And if there's anything wrong in black America, don't blame him.

SEVEN

A Quiet Victory for Emotional Justice

The First Family and the African American Psyche with Esther Armah

Black folks take great pride in the presence of three generations of African Americans in the White House. The real image of a beautiful black family beaming into the homes of all Americans has a deep impact on the psyche of the nation, and a denigrated people.—Rev. Osagyefo Uhuru Sekou[32]

Millions of Americans watched the *Cosby Show*. Week after week, season after season, Cliff and Clair Huxtable, the successful doctor and lawyer duo, effortlessly balanced successful careers, a loving relationship, a beautiful home, and a clutch of smart, erudite children without so much as a raised voice, neck roll, finger snap, or "speak to the hand" gesture. Theirs was not a world filled with concerns over layoffs, threats of home foreclosure, or finding the funds to put their children through college.

Through 1980s shoulder pads, preppy collared shirts, and crazy patterned crew-neck sweaters, this TV family offered a positive, alternative view to the often portrayed media image of the dysfunctional, disconnected black family in despair. Has the American media produced another loving black family since then?

While moving pictures on a screen released from the imagination of a script writer can go so far in changing perceptions, Clair and Cliff are no match for the real images beamed around the world of Barack, Michelle, Malia, and Sasha Obama.

Unlike the Huxtables, the Obamas do not live in a world filtered through a TV screen and live studio audience. Analysts, pundits, media outlets of all political persuasions, interest groups, and everyday people examine and opine over White House policies and President Obama's handling of key issues: unemployment, the Middle East, the wars in Afghanistan and Iraq, the environment, to name a few. For First Lady Michelle Obama, however, there are more subtle pressures attached to her role, ones that surely did not exist in the FLOTUS job-description pack of previous presidential spouses.

From day one, she has been called on to be a role model; the career woman with a strong marriage, a devoted daughter with happy children of her own. Questions fly to and fro: "is her hair chemically relaxed? Or is that a press and curl?" And black cultural observers rejoice in unison when young Malia rocks her cornrows, braids, or twist outs. The First Family is a black family that moves to the recognizable beat of African American life.

Why are these images important? Because not only are these pictures needed to mitigate the years of media images that have stereotyped black women as angry, loud, sexualized, or welfare mamas on crack, they portray the family of the president of the United States as African Americans who are comfortable being black.

Even before the First Family settled into their new life at 1600 Pennsylvania Avenue, Michelle Obama witnessed the manifestation of years of perceived notions of black womanhood. She was lambasted in the conservative press for saying, "For the first time in my adult lifetime, I'm really proud of my country."[33] Even though white American Tea Party presidential candidate Michele Bachmann made a similar assertion in August 2011, she was not raked over the coals of public opinion for being "unpatriotic."

And what about the column inches generated by the congratulatory fist-bump after Barack Obama clinched the Democratic presidential nomination in 2008? Fox News's E.D. Hill went so far as to say, "A fist bump? A pound? A terrorist fist jab? The gesture everyone seems to interpret differently."[34]

This statement in turn provided fodder for the July 21, 2008, front cover of the *New Yorker*, with a cartoon interpretation of the fist bump; an afro-topped, gun-toting Michelle Obama, clad in army fatigues and Barack looking suspiciously like Osama bin Laden (who also made a cameo in the picture). A pictorial jab at the conservative press? Or yet more fuel slung on the pyre to cremate any attempt to birth a new image of black America?

Academia and the world of research, too, have continued to deflate the place of the black woman. A March 2011 *Psychology Today* article asked, "Why are black women less physically attractive than white women?" *Are we?* Conversations with black women worldwide suggest that many of us didn't get that particular memo.

Our children are not free from the degradation; an anti abortion campaign in New York City told the world that the most dangerous place for a black child is "in the womb." And there's more. Research from the University of Michigan states that 59 percent of African American mothers had children from multiple fathers, while a 2009 study from Yale University reveals that "marriage chances for highly educated black women have declined over time relative to white women."[35]

These figures tell only one story: in cities around the world what it means to be black and the diversity of blackness are very different.

Award-winning international journalist Esther Armah has a global view on these differences. Ghana-born, London-influenced, and New York–inspired, Armah challenges men and women throughout the African Diaspora to take charge of the images of blackness and challenge the stereotypes. As a broadcaster, playwright, and producer of the successful Afrolicious Emotional Justice series, Esther Armah encourages people of color to examine how they feel about themselves and why.

We spoke just moments after she closed the mic on her morning show, *Wake Up Call* on WBAI in New York. Armah's global sensibility infuse's her thoughts on the president, the First Family, and their importance not just to African Americans, but people of color around the world.

Esther: During the presidential campaign I was sitting in my apartment in Bedford Stuyvesant in Brooklyn watching CNN, when the results for the Iowa caucus came up. I literally got up, remote in my hand, and lay on my rug in utter shock when they announced that Senator Obama had actually won Iowa. Then he became a contender that everybody paid attention to, myself included. It became not just a political race, but one that I had a stake in now, with this man, Barack Hussein Obama, who was still a virtual unknown.

Then his oratory, his charisma, and really his wife, Michelle, became part of a national and global conversation about pride and hope and change and history and excitement. It was almost as if you could taste it. It was palpable, it was infectious, it was joy-filled, and it was exciting. You felt like you became part of a global community, because even though it was the race for the president of the United States, I felt no less a part of it than my African American friends. It definitely became a union, clearly not a perfect union, but a union of sorts that went all the way through the campaign.

Joanne: The night of the election, we saw images of the new First Family in Grant Park, a family very different from any other that has made it to the White House. The images beamed around the world of two beautiful, young, African American girls, the stunning Mrs. Obama, and very handsome president-elect Obama. He was the one that people had voted for, but Obama's battle for the White House was a team effort, one that painted the African American family, and black womanhood, in a different light.

Esther: Seeing Michelle Obama fill that scene was so powerful. Often in popular culture, black women are never the heroine, never the leading lady, never the cover girl. Yet, with Barack's election, suddenly there Michelle was, all of those things. Her story speaks to the hearts and minds of every brown girl and black woman all over the world. We can look at Michelle Obama, First Lady of the United States of America, and you literally say, "Okay, that is Afro Sheen, Pink Lotion, and a flat iron. I recognize that hair. That hair is my hair. That is cocoa butter, and press powder, and ashy knees. That's who I am."

That is a profound and powerful affirmation, and it matters. It also matters that she is loved by her husband and so openly, visually so. It isn't just an affirmation of a political family, but an affirmation of a black family as an American family. The fact that she matters and she matters so much means that, as black women, we get to matter, too, in ways that we so rarely get to matter.

I call that scene a "quiet victory for emotional justice." When I say that, I mean there is a legacy of trauma, so much of it untreated, that comes from the battles that have been fought globally by black and brown folk, men and women, over all these years and through all these histories. Whether you're the child of the Independence Movement—my family is Ghanaian—whether you're coming out of the Caribbean and the Garveyite reality or the post-slavery reality coming over from the Windrush to England, whether you are coming out of the civil rights movement and you are African American, all of those things speak to particular struggles.

We bear the scars of our struggles, and I feel like every time Michelle Obama steps on that stage, the scar is less present, and the struggle less painful. There was a victory that had been scored and I had got to be a part of that. Every time President Obama chose her, I got chosen. That was significant and amazing and important. It mattered that she was not the traditional, political wife. She didn't make claims that she couldn't back up; she is educated and a mama, and a wife, and a woman. And she claims all of those.

When Michelle Obama first appeared on the cover of *Vogue*, every brown girl who had been told she was too brown, too tall, butt too big, too this, too that, got to be a cover girl too. The images are iconic and will last the test of time. Long after the presidency is over, one term or two, people will still keep those images of Michelle Obama on the front cover of *Vogue*, and the First Family *Essence* spread, and the *Time* spread, and the books, in mind. The history of those images, in the future, may be more powerful than whatever policy was or was not mastered in the time that Barack Obama was in the White House.

Joanne: Staying with Michelle for a moment, when you talk about the fascination with her, the fact that she ordinarily would not be the heroine or the chosen one, but in this story she very much is. This bears out when you take just a cursory look at the amount of material out there just on Michelle Obama. As you mentioned, the spreads in *Essence* magazine and the book *Essence* produced, *The Obamas: Portrait of America's New First Family*. There's a whole blog that's dedicated to Mrs. Obama's sartorial choices, *Mrs-O.com*. But it isn't just black women, but women across the board who are fascinated by her. Why do you think that is?

Esther: She offers a new opportunity to be in a power relationship where a woman isn't a sidekick or sitting in the backseat. She's a real partner.

I think when it comes to American family values, Michelle Obama offers American women something they haven't seen before. If you think of past First Ladies, they had a particular space and a particular role. To hear Barack Obama say, "This is my best friend, the love of my life, the rock of our family," those are not words we're used to hearing a president say, and certainly not so frequently. To see Michelle Obama stand her own ground, make her own choices, be defended when attacked, and to hear her husband talk about the importance of doing all of those things, speaks to a yearning when it comes to women and how they want to be seen in the world and how they want to be loved.

Women recognize, regardless of color, that she has had to work for what she has achieved in life. She's the brown girl that excelled, coming out of a working class family, working class roots. She's down to earth, and, for black women, she's still a "sister." We still recognize her. I still feel like we could have a drink and talk about whatever; she doesn't feel a world away from you. So she creates the sense of an accessibility to the White House that we've never necessarily seen before.

Joanne: Michelle Obama is educated and appears to have a sense of humor, but she also strongly projects her motherhood; she described her role at the White House as "Mom-in-Chief." How has she recast the often stereotypical images of black motherhood?

Esther: She's the kind of mother that we all recognize. "No. You're not going to be coddled and looked after and become a princess. You're going to have to do your own laundry and make your own breakfast."

I think it is the recognition that feels like a lens to a part of yourself that never gets revered and never gets elevated, adored or admired. Black mothers, as all mothers do, work hard for their children and their families. Through Michelle, the stereotype of us, black mothers, being "hard" is broken. Motherhood is motherhood, regardless of race.

For all of that to happen through this one woman is an extraordinary thing, and I think that when we look back at this moment in history, part of the conversation and part of the legacy will certainly be who she is and was, as much as there will be analysis about what President Obama did and didn't do in his terms in the White House.

Joanne: There's a quote I'd like to share from an article called "I'm Dreaming of a Black Christmas" written by Melissa Harris-Perry in 2009. In it she says; "Racism still exists during his presidency," that of President Obama, "and will persist when it's over. Obama cannot kill racial inequality, but he, Michelle, and the girls have altered the face of the First Family."

They've brought a warmth and a sense that even though President Obama is commander-in-chief, he's also father-in-chief. Michelle is also mom-in-chief. There's also something very traditional in having the First Lady's mother, Marian Robinson, at the White House, maintaining those extended family ties and keeping her involved in the raising of her grandchildren. Their family is like that of so many of us.

As you're holding discussions in your Emotional Justice series held in New York, what shift in attitudes are you witnessing toward the black family as a unit?

Esther: I don't know that there's been a shift. I think it's too soon to tell. But what the First Family definitely has the potential to do is resurrect the kind of love that we all seek and yearn for. The fact that the First Lady's mother, Marian, lives with them is, once again, Michelle Obama creating a family in her own image, not allowing the rules of the White House and the rules of history to dictate how she and her family lives. The First Lady wants her daughters' grandmother there. It's the first time it's really happened in the White House in recent years and it would probably take a black woman to do that. She's keeping a sense of tradition and a down-to-earthness, a groundedness, for her daughters that is really, really beautiful.

Joanne: Let's turn our attention to the president. What has Barack Obama's presence meant for black male identity?

Esther: I think there are two Baracks: the campaign Barack and President Barack. During the presidential campaign, there was the man that people got to hear and see again and again, a brother who they recognized. At the time we heard some nonsense conversations about "Is he black enough?" But the question in itself began to expand the idea of what blackness is and could be. Barack Obama is a man born of Kenyan parentage, so he's of African ancestry and of Kansas ancestry through his mother. He's a diasporic black man, as well as an African American black man.

The kind of man that he is prompted all of these conversations within African American spaces, but to me, I just recognized him from the diaspora, from the continent, and felt that what he offered was an expansion in our conversation about black identity. We needed to have that, and his presence enabled that and continues to enable that in ways that probably haven't even been documented yet. I think that's an important and significant contribution.

Joanne: And of his marriage to Michelle?

Esther: The fact that he is a brother who chose a black woman, for black men, was such an affirmation as well. He chose within his own community when it came to love and lifelong partnership. His little girls look like little brown girls all across the world. You recognize them. Again, curlers and Afro Sheen going in that hair are markers we recognize.

Yet who Obama has become as a president and commander in chief of the United States is a different kind of black man. For many brothers there was a disappointment in him not being the type of man that they would aspire to be; they aspired to the Barack in the presidential campaign, especially in terms of his family life, but *not* Barack the president.

Thoughts are also colored by what his policies have and have not achieved, and how he's handled various issues, such as mass incarceration, policy brutality, and the economy. There has often been the conversation about whether Obama has ever been angry enough about issues that afflict black people. Has he ever really done enough to pursue the agendas and the interests of African Americans?

Joanne: I wonder though, Esther, if it's more complex than it just being a disappointment with a lack of policy focused on African American communities? In Rev. Osagyefo Uhuru Sekou's May 2011 article entitled "Cornel West and the Crisis of Black Leadership," he makes the point that black leadership has often been formed in retaliation to "the white man." But that dynamic shifted dramatically when the person in power, the person in the White House, was no longer white, but black. Is that where the disappointment you mention comes in? The game has changed, and no one is yet sure of the rules?

Esther: I think that's a powerful observation. There is no question that Barack becoming president of the United States meant that we were going to have to make a litmus shift in terms of how we define and see power, and that partially, the problem has been this one-dimensional focus on power.

There has been a conversation, when it comes to the United States of America, surrounding a preoccupation with how black people are seen in the eyes of white people, because of the continuum of history connecting slavery, Jim Crow, the black freedom movement, the women's civil rights movement, and beyond.

The power conversation and the power dynamic has been black and white. Once you put a black man in the White House the power dynamic shifts. That's a great shift, because it means we are pushed and forced to grow and to expand, and to think about the nuance and the different ways in which power manifests.

That's been part of the challenge for President Obama during his time in office. All the different African American commentators and their critiques of him are personal. We heard, on the one hand, really severe critique, and on the other, completely blindfolded praise. He is worthy of neither.

There is almost a possessiveness and a protectiveness that we, as black people, feel about him because we understand the world in which he lives, but I think it's also about us negotiating and navigating a more complicated, sophisticated relationship with power that's not a pure black-white dynamic. The fact of him being president forces us, whether we like it or not, to explore that. You saw it with Cornel West and Tavis Smiley with their Poverty Tour and you hear it with comments by folks like Steve Harvey, Tom Joyner, and Rev. Al Sharpton, both the criticism and the praise.

The criticism and the praise has been set up as a conversation of the civil rights type of leadership verses this moment of leadership, because Barack's presidency was unexpected. Nobody thought he could actually get there. Part of that conversation became, how will a black presidency impact traditional black leadership? I think it's the navigation of that, which has been part of the problem and is still being navigated. The *nuance* of that is still being navigated and that's a really good thing. We need to interrogate our relationship with power and internalize it more, which I think comes back to the issue of emotional justice. The part of what needs to be challenged is who we are to one another, who we've been, and who we want to continue to be to white people.

Maybe that's exactly where it's supposed to go. The nature of the conversation and the nature of the struggle shifts, and that's an important move.

Joanne: You touched on comments made by Cornel West, and there was one that stood out to me when he described the president as a "black mascot of Wall Street oligarchs and a black puppet of corporate plutocrats." There's a level of familiarity, almost brotherly-ness we witness in the way President Obama is referred to and commented upon. There's a connection that is expected but which he cannot be fully party to. Is there a way that we have to, through this presidency, mature in our outlook of how we operate with power and, at times, give our power and agency away to others, in a "Great. You're there, you go handle it," manner?

Esther: More than one critique can be true at the same time. Somebody can be personally offended by how they've been treated and their critique of the president be valid. Each critique has validity. One can be dismissed as not being relevant to the conversation, but the critique still has merit. I think there's no question we're being asked to mature in how we navigate those who are in power, because so much of what Barack Obama's apparent failure has been about is our expectation of what he has the potential to do but has not done or is perceived to not have done, so far. That actually is not, to me, a conversation about Barack Obama. It's a conversation persistently about our insistence on creating messiahs out of people and putting folks on pedestals when they should be with the people in the streets. The insistence on doing that has been a major part of the problem.

It can't keep being the conversation that it's always been, but this presidency, this is a situation that forces us to reassess the discussion, and I actually think that's a great thing. It's much needed, but it's complicated, and it's challenging, and it's personal in a lot of ways, so that people want to take the higher ground, the authentic ground. All the grounds are in the mix to be messed with because that's the reality of having a black man in the White House.

He's in a house that was built, to a large degree, by the forced labor of enslaved people of African descent. There are all these moments of history that rub together and stand on top of each other, and when you come down to it, it's actually about black people's relationship with power. That needs to

178

fundamentally shift so that you're always in pursuit of your own interests and you don't stop pursuing them until you get what it is you and your folks need. Even that is not as simple as the statement sounds, but what it does mean is that this expectation that somebody's going to take better care of you because they look like you, is a fallacy that's been proven wrong many, many, many times.

Every president lets the people down. That's inevitable. The question is how we insist that power hear us, respond to us. And that, historically, involves our relationship as black people with white people and expanding that so that it becomes our relationship with ourselves, with our own communities and with our own agendas, and how are we making sure that those are being pursued in ways that honor where we want to go. And where they're not, you keep elevating your voice until they are.

Joanne: And we saw that to great effect with the debt-ceiling crisis in August 2011. Tea Partiers dug their heels in and said, "Listen, we don't want to raise the debt ceiling. We were voted in on this basis and we're going to keep our promise to our voters."

At the time there was talk about invoking a particular element of the Fourteenth Amendment, offering President Obama the ultimate power to raise the debt ceiling and veto what everybody else had to say. What struck me as interesting at the time was the expectation that he should be a bulldog and assert his authority forcefully.

He didn't, choosing instead to continue on the path of consensus and compromise. How does his awareness of how black men are perceived impact on how he conducts himself?

Esther: He appears fully mindful of how black men are perceived, but also he has been persistent in his willingness to come to the table and to make compromise far and beyond what anybody wants him to do. He has done so at his peril. He has made it, he believes, an important part of his presidency and he's maintained that. I think the refusal to invoke the Fourteenth Amendment, whilst it would have been an indication of a president, a commander-in-chief, taking control, it would have been out of character with the President Obama who has almost unfailingly been about concession to his opponents.

There's no question he would have been critiqued whatever he had done, but I think that there's no question that he's aware of how black men are perceived. But there's also, to me, no question that that was not the only thing that he was thinking about because, consistently, he has been the man that comes to the table and says, "Let's talk. Let's compromise. Let's work together."

Being measured and thoughtful and wanting to hear from all different sides, that's who he appears to be and what he brings to politics. However, there's only so much compromise that is productive and progressive when nobody compromises other than you.

Joanne: I have a quote here that says, "The way in which African American people make meaning for themselves inside the American Empire has been recast."[36] That was in an article reflecting on the election of President Obama. What thoughts come to mind when you hear that?

Esther: Belonging. That black people, African Americans, have always been the outsiders, the undesired, looking for a way in, to be considered, to be included. From being considered three-sixths of a human being, to the fight to have the Constitution even include their humanity, the fight from bondage into some kind of freedom has always been from outside positions of power. I think with the 2008 presidential campaign there was a deep shift to a new sense of belonging.

What I heard again and again was folks saying, "I am an American," or "I am proud to be American," because there was, in that moment, a powerful sense of belonging.

Joanne: Obama's win was felt throughout the African diaspora. We've talked about how the presence of the Obamas has impacted African American notions of identity, but what about elsewhere?

Esther: The impact is twofold. I'm Ghanaian. My mother is Ashanti. When I speak to her on the phone she'll ask, "How are you? How are things doing?" And she'll always ask, "How is my son?" I have a brother, so when she first said that I assumed she was talking about my brother. She meant Barack Obama.

There were prayer circles for Barack Obama in churches in Ghana and all across Africa. There is a protectiveness toward him on the continent because his father is Kenyan. The disappointment in terms of the policy hasn't permeated that protectiveness that folks like my mother and her generation feels. My mother is almost eighty years old now and there's definitely a willingness to continue to push and encourage and cajole him in the direction of greatness because they believe that's absolutely what he's supposed to do. There's still a belief that there are things that he's willing or going to do for the continent of Africa that nobody else can do.

All mistaken, if you ask me. All mistaken. There's no evidence that suggests that any of that is true, but that belief, which is as strong as my disagreement with it, is 100 percent there.

African people claim him as theirs and feel that there is now a connection between American and Africa that there has never been and there is a conversation from America to Africa that is different than it ever was.

Joanne: Why do you think he won't do anything? Is it an unwillingness on his part, or because people, just like here, aren't pushing him to do anything in Africa?

Esther: I think he's doing in Africa what other U.S. presidents before him have done, and I think just as for African Americans over here, that if Africa wants him to do anything more than what he is doing, it would require a very particular, specific pressure for that to happen. In that sense, he is an American president, not a black president. His policy is not so far away from what has gone before, insofar as nothing major has happened in a positive sense.

Yet, his trip to Ghana was the equivalent of when the Black Stars almost won the World Cup. Hugely significant! The symbolic significance of him choosing to go *home*, which is what I still call Africa, should never be underestimated. Nor should how little he has accomplished policy-wise be underestimated.

Sometimes I would argue that we are too big on symbol

and culture, and ignore the pragmatic, social justice, sharp lens focus and resolution that is really required. We give him far too much leeway for his particular brand of oratory to soothe our souls and take us home with warm hearts, when nothing has changed from the day before he came into office until today.

Joanne: How concerned are you that the Obama presidency's biggest contribution to African Americans will be primarily symbolic?

Esther: Don't underestimate the power of symbol. In a country that was founded with African people in chains, the reality of a black man occupying the epitome of white power should never be underestimated. There are many folks who say now, based on their disappointment over policy, "Yeah. He was elected. And what?"

I say, "No." The power of that moment should never be underestimated, and I think, historically, it may not be. When you're living in the moment of someone's presidency you're occupied with a present of what they are or what they are not doing. But that campaign and those moments literally brought a country, a world, to its feet; without exception, turned an entire world's focus on one man; changed for a moment the way the world thought of America, and brought conversations about race to a platform and an agenda that had never been heard on that level and in that way.

There were all kinds of flaws in all of that, but the symbolic power of what it represented should never be underestimated, and I certainly will never underestimate it. It's different than the reality of governing a nation in two wars, with an economy in crisis, with an extraordinary unemployment rate, and a bipartisan political philosophy that is absolutely addicted to ensuring that this president gets nothing done.

Add to that, the elevation of a certain nationalism that really just shields racism, when you have a certain portion of the American population that feels and says, "We need to take America back," as if the fact of a black president means something has been taken away from them.

The significance of his presidency is indelible: the existential fact of his being elected, and the image of Michelle and the two girls, hand-in-hand walking down Grant Park and being introduced to the cheering crowds with the words, "Welcome to the First Family," is historically unprecedented. Never underestimate that.

Joanne: The Obama daughters have been another source of powerful symbolism during this presidency. The relationship that the president has with them is clearly one that's very engaged and loving, and seeing it is powerful. There are other powerful symbols too, like the Obama's older daughter, Malia, wearing her hair in twists and in braids. It's like it gave other black girls in the United States permission to wear their natural hair; a powerful statement, so simply made.

Esther: Affirmation. Global, world stage, overwhelming affirmation. It became the style. Malia and Sasha had their own accidental iconic moment. The fact that that nappy hair, sometimes the focus of pain and hurt and rage and rejection and trauma, was for a moment a sign of beauty and sweetness and being adorable. It brought grown women to tears. And the fact that they have a mother who has her daughters wearing their hair in natural styles, all of these things matter and impact our society and culture.

That's what I mean when I say that the symbolism of those things should never be underestimated; when you've had an entire history of those images of black hair in its natural state being ascribed to ugliness or being problematic or difficult, which is so often how Afro hair is described. To see that beauty, that culture, embodied in the First Family is a powerful affirmation. If it's okay for them, trust me, it's going to be okay for some other people.

That notion alone says something about our psyche and our sensibility. Affirmation matters. If it didn't, advertisers would not spend millions and millions and millions of dollars trying to convince us otherwise. For the First Family to embody that is really special and precious, and will have its own long-lasting space in the national psyche.

GOING FORWARD

A time comes when silence is betrayal.—Dr. Martin Luther King Jr., 1967

"History," said Malcolm X, "is a people's memory, and without a memory, man is demoted to the lower animals." History arms us with knowledge, context and foresight; understanding the struggles of the past empowers us to script our own future as free and self-determined human beings.

As I write, a new memorial in honor of Dr. Martin Luther King Jr. is being officially dedicated in Washington, DC. Above the stone statue and the sound of the crowds and speeches, I cannot help but hear King's own voice ring out—"silence is betrayal"—words that continue to resonate so loudly decades after he uttered them during his renowned "Beyond Vietnam" speech.

Have *we* been too silent?

Lulled into a satisfied slumber by the election of the first black man to serve as commander-in-chief and president of the United States of America, have we handed over our voice and agency to others to act on our behalf?

As individuals and communities, have we slackened in

our responsibility to deepen the democratic process and abolish racial injustice in all its forms?

Isn't *now* the time, more than ever, to stand up and organize—not just for our own right to life, liberty, and the pursuit of happiness, but in solidarity with those less fortunate than us, those struggling against the oppressive silence imposed by poverty, lack of education, and resident status?

Can we begin to redefine black power as the struggle to apply the lessons of our own history to the liberation and transformation of American society as a whole?

Can we begin to speak of an inclusive "democracy of color," a democracy of transformation and justice for the 99 percent?

The Redefining Black Power project will continue to grow and evolve as it has during the very process of making this book; questions moved beyond the initial euphoria surrounding the 2008 election to deep-rooted and complex intergenerational concerns of African Americans regarding the freedom struggle, law, media, opportunity, health, equality, representation, family, community, and movement building. Part of the story is how the conversation transformed from "what can President Obama do for us?" to "what can we do for ourselves?"

This is a time of global democratic awakening; a time of reclaiming our voices, our finances, our agency, our rights, and our full civic power. Last spring, protestors across the Arab-speaking world revolted against injustice in their dictator-controlled countries. In the heat of the summer, the wave of protest spread to youth in the UK who took to the streets, outraged at the killing of a black man at the hands of police, and the stinging cuts to social services, education, and employment opportunities.

With the arrival of autumn, the wave of protest made it across the Atlantic to the United States. The Occupy Wall Street movement emerged in New York and took hold in a multitude of cities across the country. "This is not about left versus right," said twenty-five-year-old photographer Christopher Walsh, from Bushwick, Brooklyn. "It's about hierarchy versus autonomy."[37]

The dedication of the MLK memorial isn't the only thing happening this weekend. As if timed to sync with the event, protests erupted in more than 150 cities to demand an end to injustice and the absence of economic accountability in the United States.

In the nonviolent tradition of Henry David Thoreau and Martin Luther King, thousands have been arrested committing civil disobedience, including Dr. Cornel West, and the numbers continue to multiply daily. "Democracy is not for sale," read one banner. "If you're not angry, you're not paying attention," read another. "I woke up in a sweat from the American Dream," read the sign of one Times Square protestor. Thousands chanted, "I'm not moving," and "This is what democracy looks like!" The 99 percent is speaking out powerfully against the irrevocable damage caused by a handful of financial power brokers; the 1 percent dictating the economic fortunes of most of us.

This public push back, this outcry, this demand from "we the people" may in the end be the best thing for both black America and the Obama presidency. In 2008, Obama's battle cry was "yes *we* can," never "yes *I* can." Have the rest of us been too caught up in symbolism of what we *thought* was the realization of Dr. King's dream to get the revelation and get involved?

Big questions remain. What will this time in history mean for the development of civic consciousness across color lines? Will we once again uncover the spirit of the black freedom movement and push toward the continuous evolution of a just society?

This time, this moment we live in places a spotlight on all of us to do our part, carry our share and spread the load. The Obama presidency has been and will continue to be historic for people of color and the nation, but what matters is what we do during this time and space of opportunity, uprising, and change. Will we sit back and wait for someone to do the work for us or we will we take it to the world like Harriet Tubman, Fannie Lou Hamer, and Rosa Parks?

In the moments before he was arrested committing nonviolent civil disobedience on the steps of the U.S. Supreme Court today, Cornel West said to us all: "We're here to bear witness with, to be in solidarity with the Occupy movement all around the world, because we love poor people, we love working people, and we want Martin Luther King, Jr., to smile from the grave that we haven't forgot his movement."[38]

We've got work to do.

Let's do it together.

Joanne Griffith,
www.redefiningblackpower.com
October 2011

ACKNOWLEDGMENTS

The Redefining Black Power project would not exist without the time, energy, and enthusiasm of so many people. I am truly humbled and, without wishing to sound like an Oscar acceptance speech, would like to acknowledge the following:

God: thank you for leading me here. Brian DeShazor, director of the Pacifica Radio Archives: who would have thought a chance visit to KPFK would lead us here? Thank you for your friendship and entrusting me with your vision. Greg Ruggiero, editor at City Lights Books: your passion, expertise, way with words, and guidance have been invaluable to me throughout this journey. Muchas gracias, amigo. The Pacifica Radio Archives staff: Mark Torres, Edgar Toledo, Mariana Berkovich, Shawn Dellis, Haunani Singer, and the Pacifica Radio Archives Preservation and Access coordinator, Adi Gevins; Lawrence Ferlinghetti, Elaine Katzenberger, and Stacey Lewis of City Lights Books; to all the contributors interviewed as part of this project, thank you for your time and dedication to social change: Dr. Molefi Asante, Dr. Julianne Malveaux, Dr. Michelle Alexander, Ramona Africa, Van Jones, Rev. Dr. Jeremiah Wright, Dr. Vincent Harding, Esther Armah, Linn Washington Jr., and Marc Lamont Hill, Melissa Harris-Perry; to the Pacifica Radio network producers, hosts, and contributors who brought life to the first phase of Redefining Black Power, especially Esther Manilla, Aimee Allison, Mark Bamuhti Joseph, Minister Christopher Muhammad, Dereca Blackman. Gloria Minott, Jonetta Rose Barris, Karen Spellman, Margaret Prescod, Lucia Chappelle, Nana Gyamfi, Karume James, Frank Wilderson, Jasmyne Cannick, Ron Buckmire, Sabiha Khan, Myra Jimenez, Jordan Monroe, and Jennifer Obakhume; to the Pacifica Radio network stations: KPFA 94.1 FM (Berkeley), KPFK 90.7 FM (Los Angeles), WBAI 99.5 FM (New York), KPFT 90.1 FM (Houston), and WPFW 89.9 FM (Washington, DC), thank you for supporting this project and the vital work of the Pacifica Radio Archives; to the team at George Blood Audio in Philadelphia: this work is only possible because of your dedication to preservation. to the best team of transcribers who transformed the audio into the written word: Lainie Lorde, Donna Walker, Natalie Yahr, and Allison Fussell Louie; to my dear friends Natalie Davies Ridgeway, Dee Patterson, and Christabel Nsiah-Buadi: thank you for listening (a lot!)

Special acknowledgements go to my parents, Gloria Griffith and George Griffith. Thank you for showing me how to tackle life's injustices with grace, fortitude, integrity, and an open heart. To my sisters, Juliet Richards and Annette Griffith. See, your little sister's talking is being put to good use! Continue to let your light shine, beautiful ones. All of the Griffith/Richards/Jones crew: we are small in number, but mighty in deed!

To my husband and best friend, Maurice Poplar. Dr. King led a movement and my curiosity in him led me to you and the adventure of our lives. You believe in me more than

I do myself, but I could do none of this without you. Thank you for being you and letting me be me, my love.

And to you the reader and listeners: thank you for supporting the Pacifica Radio Archives and taking part in this journey. We are all the victories of the struggle.

NOTES

1. U.S. Bureau of the Census, *Voting and Registration in the Election of November 2008* (Washington, DC: Bureau of the Census, 2010), http://www.census.gov/hhes/www/socdemo/voting/publications/p20/2008/.
2. PolitiFact, "The Obameter: Tracking Obama's Campaign Promises," http://www.politifact.com/truth-o-meter/promises/obameter/.
3. U.S. Bureau of the Census, *Income, Poverty, and Health Insurance Coverage in the United States: 2010* (Washington, DC: Bureau of the Census, 2011), http://www.census.gov/prod/2011pubs/p60-239.pdf.
4. U.S. Bureau of Labor Statistics, *Employment Status of the Civilian Population by Race, Sex, and Age* (Washington, DC: U.S. Bureau of Labor Statistics, 2011), http://www.bls.gov/news.release/empsit.t02.htm.
5. Jonathan Allen, "Maxine Waters to Obama on Unemployment: Treat Blacks like Iowans," *Politico*, September 8, 2011, http://www.politico.com/news/stories/0911/62979.html.
6. Office of Congresswoman Maxine Waters, "Waters Asks President Obama to Target Jobs Proposals to Aid Hardest Hit Communities, Including Communities with High Rates of Unemployed African Americans," news release, September 8, 2011, http://www.waters.house.gov/News/DocumentSingle.aspx?DocumentID=258774.
7. Kwame Anthony Appiah and Henry Louis Gates Jr., eds., *Africana: Civil Rights: An A-Z Reference of the Movement That Changed America* (Philadelphia: Running Press, 2004), 373
8. Clarence Lusane, *The Black History of the White House* (San Francisco: City Lights Books, 2010), 15.
9. Sabrina Tavernise, "Recession Study Finds Hispanics Hit the Hardest," *New York Times*, July 26, 2011.
10. Michelle Alexander, *The New Jim Crow: Mass Incarceration in the Age of Colorblindness* (New York: The New Press, 2010), 2.
11. The Schott Foundation for Public Education, *Yes We Can: The*

Schott 50 State Report on Public Education and Black Males (Cambridge, MA: The Schott Foundation for Public Education, 2010), http://blackboysreport.org/bbreport.pdf.

12. The Annie E. Casey Foundation, *2011 Kids Count Data Book* (Baltimore: The Annie E. Casey Foundation, 2011), http://datacenter.kidscount.org/databook/2011/OnlineBooks/2011KCDB_FINAL.pdf.

13. Center for Responsible Lending, *Foreclosures by Race and Ethnicity: The Demographics of a Crisis* (Durham, NC: Center for Responsible Lending, 2010), http://www.responsiblelending.org/mortgage-lending/research-analysis/foreclosures-by-race-and-ethnicity.pdf.

14. Beth T. Bates, " 'Double V for Victory' Mobilizes Black Detroit, 1941–1946," in *Freedom North: Black Freedom Struggles Outside the South, 1940–1980*, ed. Jeanne Theoharis and Komozi Woodard (New York: Palgrave Macmillian, 2003), 18.

15. Martin Luther King Jr., *"Beyond Vietnam: A Time to Break Silence"* (speech, Riverside Church, New York, NY, April 4, 1967).

16. Vincent Harding, *"The Religion of Black Power," in The Religious Situation: 1968*, ed. Donald Cutler (Boston: Beacon Press, 1968), 2–3.

17. Clayborne Carson and Kris Shepard, eds., *A Call to Conscience: The Landmark Speeches of Dr. Martin Luther King, Jr.* (New York: Warner Books, 2001).

18. W. E. B. DuBois, *The Souls of Black Folk* (New York: Modern Library, 2003).

19. Amy Jacques-Garvey, ed., *Philosophy and Opinions of Marcus Garvey* (Phoenix, AZ: *The Journal of Pan African Studies*, 2009), e-book, 31.

20. Sabrina Tavernise, "U.S. Poverty Rate, 1 in 6, at Highest Level in Years," *New York Times*, September 13, 2011, http://www.truth-out.org/us-poverty-rate-1-6-highest-level-years/1315931339.

21. U.S. Bureau of Labor Statistics, *"Employment Situation: February 2009,"* news release, February 2009, http://www.bls.gov/news.release/archives/empsit_03062009.pdf.

22. Velma Hart, CNBC-sponsored town hall meeting, Washington, DC, September 20, 2011.

23. U.S. Bureau of Labor Statistics, "Data Retrieval: Labor Force Statistics (CPS)—Household Data—Table A-15. Alternative Measures of Labor Underutilization," http://www.bls.gov/webapps/legacy/cpsatab15.htm. U6 represents the "total unemployed, plus all persons marginally attached to the labor force, plus total employed part time for economic reasons, as a percent of the civilian labor force plus all persons marginally attached to the labor force."

24. Mariko Chang, *Lifting as We Climb: Women of Color, Wealth, and America's Future* (Oakland, CA: The Insight Center for Community Economic Development, 2010), 3.

25. *Rick Edmonds, Emily Guskin, and Tom Rosenstiel, "Newspapers: Missed the 2010 Media Rally," in The State of the News Media: An Annual Report on American Journalism (Washington, DC: Pew Research Center's Project for Excellence in Journalism, 2011),* http://stateofthemedia.org/2011/newspapers-essay/.

26. U.S. Constitution, amend. 1, "Congress shall make no law respecting an establishment of religion, or prohibiting the free exercise thereof; or abridging the freedom of speech, or of the press; or the right of the people peaceably to assemble, and to petition the Government for a redress of grievances," http://www.archives.gov/exhibits/charters/bill_of_rights_transcript.html.

27. Paul Farhi, "White House Video Blog Offers an Inside View," *Washington Post*, May 15, 2010, http://www.washingtonpost.com/wp-dyn/content/article/2010/05/14/AR2010051401316.html.

28. Mayhill Fowler, "Obama: No Surprise That Hard-Pressed Pennsylvanians Turn Bitter," *Huffington Post*, April 11, 2008, http://www.huffingtonpost.com/mayhill-fowler/obama-no-surprise-that-ha_b_96188.html.

29. Andy Birkey, "Bachmann: Blaming Minority Lending for Economic Crisis 'Does Not Mean I'm a Racist,' " *Minnesota Independent*, September 29, 2008, http://minnesotaindependent.com/10758/bachmann-blaming-minority-lending-for-economic-crisis-does-not-mean-im-a-racist.

30. Kirwan Institute for the Study of Race and Ethnicity, "Chart 4. Federal ARRA Contract Procurements by Race of Recipient Business Owner," in *Race-Recovery Index: How Have Communities of Color Been Impacted by Two Years of Stimulus?* (Columbus, OH: Kirwan Institute for the Study of Race and Ethnicity, 2011), http://4909e99d35cada6 3e7f757471b7243be73e53e14.gripelements.com/publications/race-recovery_feb2011.pdf

31. Patrick E. Tyler, "A New Power In the Streets," *New York Times*, February 17, 2003, 1.

32. Osagyefo Uhuru Sekou, "Cornel West and the Crisis in Black Leadership," *Feminist Wire*, May 20, 2011.

33. Michelle Obama, campaign rally speech, Madison, Wisconsin, February 18, 2008.

34. E. D. Hill, *America's Pulse*, Fox News, June 6, 2008.

35. Natalie Nitsche and Hannah Brueckner, *Opting out of the family? Social Change in Racial Inequality in Family Formation Patterns and Marriage Outcomes among Highly Educated Women* (New Haven, CT: Center for Research on Inequalities and the Life Course, 2009).

36. Sekou, "Cornel West."

37. N. R. Kleinfield and Cara Buckley, "Wall Street Occupiers, Protesting Till Whenever," *New York Times*, September 30, 2011, http://www.nytimes.com/2011/10/01/nyregion/wall-street-occupiers-protesting-till-whenever.html?_r=2&pagewanted=1&sq=occupy%20wall%20 street&st=cse&scp=3.
38. Jorge Rivas, "Occupy Wall Street Protests Go Global While Focus Stays on the Poor," Colorlines.com, October 17, 2011, http:// colorlines.com/archives/2011/10/weekend_update_occupy_wall_ street_demonstrations.html.

SELECTED BIBLIOGRAPHY AND AUDIO REFERENCES

Ben Agger, *The Sixties at 40: Leaders and Activists Remember & Look Forward* (Boulder, CO: Paradigm Publishers, 2009).

Michelle Alexander, *The New Jim Crow: Mass Incarceration in the Age of Colorblindness* (The New Press, 2010).

Kwame Anthony Appiah and Henry Louis Gates Jr., eds., *Africana: Civil Rights: An A-Z Reference of the Movement That Changed America* (Philadelphia: Running Press, 2004).

Molefi Kete Asante, *Afrocentricity: The Theory of Social Change* (Trenton, NJ: Africa World Press, 1988).

Molefi Kete Asante, *Erasing Racism: The Survival of the American Nation* (Amherst, NY: Prometheus Books, 2009).

Beth T. Bates, " 'Double V for Victory' Mobilizes Black Detroit, 1941–1946," in *Freedom North: Black Freedom Struggles Outside the South, 1940–1980*, ed. Jeanne Theoharis and Komozi Woodard (New York: Palgrave Macmillian, 2003).

Derrick Bell, *Faces at the Bottom of the Well: The Permanence of Racism* (New York: Basic Books, 1992).

Stokely Carmichael and Charles V. Hamilton, *Black Power: The Politics of Liberation in America* (New York: Vintage Books, 1967).

Clayborne Carson and Kris Shepard, eds., *A Call to Conscience: The Landmark Speeches of Dr. Martin Luther King, Jr.* (New York: Warner Books, 2001).

Ward Churchill and Jim Vander Wall, *Agents of Repression: The FBI's Secret Wars Against the Black Panther Party and the American Indian Movement* (Cambridge, MA: South End Press, 1988).

James H. Cone, *Martin & Malcolm & America: A Dream or a Nightmare* (Maryknoll, NY: Orbis Books, 1992).

Constance Curry, *Silver Rights: The Story of the Carter Family's Brave Decision to Send Their Children to an All-White School and Claim Their Civil Rights* (New York: Harvest Books, 1995).

Angela Davis, *Angela Davis: An Autobiography* (New York: International Publishers, 1989).

Frederick Douglass, *Narrative of The Life of Frederick Douglass, An American Slave, Written By Himself: A New Critical Edition*, ed. Angela Y. Davis (San Francisco: City Lights Books, 2010).

Frederick Douglass, *"West India Emancipation"* (speech, Canandaigua, NY, August 3, 1857), http://www.lib.rochester.edu/index.cfm?PAGE=4398.

W. E. B. DuBois, *The Souls of Black Folk* (New York: Modern Library, 2003).

Lani Guinier and Gerald Torres, *The Miner's Canary: Enlisting Race, Resisting Power, Transforming Democracy* (Cambridge, MA: Harvard University Press, 2002).

Vincent Harding, *Martin Luther King: The Inconvenient Hero* (Maryknoll, NY: Orbis Books, 2008).

John Heilemann and Mark Halperin, *Game Change: Obama and the Clintons, McCain and Palin, and the Race of a Lifetime* (New York: HarperCollins, 2010).

Van Jones, *The Green Collar Economy: How One Solution Can Fix Our Two Biggest Problems* (New York: HarperCollins, 2008).

Peniel E. Joseph, "Black Studies, Student Activism, and the Black Power Movement," in *The Black Power Movement: Rethinking the Civil Rights–Black Power Era*, ed. Peniel E. Joseph (New York: Routledge, 2006).

Clarence Lusane, *The Black History of the White House* (San Francisco: City Lights Books, 2010).

Manning Marable, *Malcolm X: A Life of Reinvention* (New York: Viking, 2011).

John Meany, *Has The Civil Rights Movement Been Successful?* (North Mankato, MN: Heinemann, 2009).

Mark A. Noll, *God and Race in American Politics: A Short History* (Princeton, NJ: Princeton University Press, 2010).

Barack Obama, *The Audacity of Hope: Thoughts on Reclaiming the American Dream* (New York: Vintage, 2008).

200

Barack Obama, *Dreams from my Father: A Story of Race and Inheritance* (New York: Crown, 2007).

Benjamin Quarles, *Black Abolitionists* (New York: Oxford University Press, 1969).

Jane Rhodes, *Framing the Black Panthers: The Spectacular Rise of a Black Power Icon* (New York: The New Press, 2007).

Noliwe M. Rooks, *White Money, Black Power: The Surprising History of African American Studies and the Crisis of Race in Higher Education* (Boston: Beacon, 2006).

R. Drew Smith, ed., *New Day Begun: African American Churches and Civic Culture in Post–Civil Rights America*, vol. 1 of *The Public Influences of African American Churches* (Durham, NC: Duke University Press, 2003).

R. Drew Smith, ed., *Long March Ahead: African American Churches and Public Policy in Post–Civil Rights America*, vol. 2 of *The Public Influences of African American Churches* (Durham, NC: Duke University Press, 2004).

James Tackach, *The Civil Rights Movement* (Farmington Hills, MI: Greenhaven Press, 2001).

Quintard Taylor, *America I AM Black Facts: The Timelines of African American History, 1601–2008* (New York: SmileyBooks, 2009).

Stephen Tuck, *We Ain't What We Ought To Be: The Black Freedom Struggle from Emancipation to Obama* (Cambridge, MA: Harvard University Press, 2010).

Joe Wood, ed., *Malcolm X: In Our Own Image* (New York: St. Martin's Press, 1992).

Jeremiah A. Wright, Jr., *A Sankofa Moment: The History of Trinity United Church of Christ* (Dallas, TX: Saint Paul Press, 2010).

SELECT AUDIO SOURCES

James Baldwin, *After the Murder of Four Children*, speech at the New York Community Church, 1963, BB0873.

H. Rap Brown and Stokely Carmichael, *Speech on Black Political Action: An address to the Black Panthers*, February 1968, B4532.

Stokely Carmichael, *Discussion of the Civil Rights Movement*, interviewed by Terence Cannon, 1966, BB0720.

Shirley Chisholm, *Campaign Speeches*, interview by Miriam Rosen, 1972, BC0830.

Kathleen Cleaver, *Interview with Kathleen Cleaver*, Minister of

201

Information of the Black Panther Party (and *Eldridge Cleaver's wife) discusses Black activism and her husband's activities*, interviewed by Julius Lester, 1968, BB3788.02.

Angela Davis, *Statement by Angela Davis*, 1971, BB4136.

W.E.B. DuBois, *A Recording of W. E. B. DuBois' Own View of Himself*, 1964, BB1295.

Fannie Lou Hamer, *The Life of Fannie Lou Hamer*, 1977, KZ0108.

Florynce Kennedy, *Trial By Sex*, 1968, BB3200.

Elijah Muhammad, *An Interview with Elijah Muhammad*, interviewed by Charles Hobson, 1968, BB3099.

Huey P. Newton, *An Interview with Huey P. Newton*, produced and narrated by Colin Edwards, 1968, BB1637.

Rosa Parks, *Commentary of a Black Southern Bus Rider*; interviewed by Sidney Roger, 1962, BB0566.

Paul Robeson, *Paul Robeson: World Citizen*, interviewed by Elsa Knight Thompson and Harold Winkler, 1958, BB0534.

Malcolm X, *A Choice of Two Roads, Malcolm X and Bayard* Rustin, moderated by John Donald, 1960, BB3014.

PACIFICA RADIO ARCHIVES COLLECTIONS

Voices of Pacifica: Defining Black Power, 2001, PZ0468.

Mississippi Freedom Summer, 1981, KZ1055.

Women of the Civil Rights Movement, PZ0667 a-f.

The Black Panthers Collection, PZ0728 a-f.

Malcolm X 1925–1965, 2001, PZ0446.

ABOUT THE EDITOR

Joanne Griffith is an award-winning international broadcast journalist who has reported, produced, and hosted programs for the British Broadcasting Corporation, National Public Radio, and the Pacifica Radio Network.

Joanne has spent her career telling the stories of tragedy and triumph throughout the African diaspora; from voting rights in the United States, the legacy of slavery in the Caribbean, the contribution of immigrants to the United Kingdom, and the politics of food and power in southern Africa.

Now based in Los Angeles, Joanne hosts a weekly radio program based on the historic audio held in the Pacifica Radio Archives for BBC Radio.

Redefining Black Power is her first book.

ABOUT THE CONTRIBUTORS

Ramona Africa
Ramona Africa is a political prisoner and minister of communication for MOVE, a revolutionary organization founded by John Africa with a focus on natural law. Ramona Africa is the sole adult survivor of the Philadelphia Police Department's May 13, 1985, bombing of a residential home in Philadelphia.

A law graduate of Temple University, Ramona Africa has been an integral part of MOVE for over thirty years. She travels the world sharing the work and mission of MOVE.

Professor Michelle Alexander

Michelle Alexander is a highly acclaimed civil rights lawyer, advocate, and legal scholar who currently holds a joint appointment at the Kirwan Institute for the Study of Race and Ethnicity and the Moritz College of Law at Ohio State University. Prior to joining the Kirwan Institute, Alexander was an associate professor of law at Stanford Law School, where she directed the Civil Rights Clinics. For several years, Professor Alexander also served as the director of the Racial Justice Program for the ACLU of Northern California, which spearheaded a national campaign against racial profiling by law enforcement. In 2005, Michelle Alexander won a Soros Justice Fellowship, which supported the writing of her first book, *The New Jim Crow: Mass Incarceration in the Age of Colorblindness*.

Esther Armah

Esther Armah is a radio and television host, playwright, and award-winning international journalist. In New York, she hosts *Wake Up Call*, WBAI 99.5 FM's morning show, and is a regular commentator and guest host on *GRITtv with Laura Flanders* and a local public access program, *Ancestor House with Camille Yarbrough*. Esther has written extensively on African diaspora issues for the *Guardian*, *Essence*, and *West Africa*. The themes of her written work are reflected in the issues portrayed in Armah's four New York stage plays, *Can I Be Me?*, *Forgive Me?*, *Entitled!*, and *SAVIOUR?* Esther is the creator and moderator of *Afrolicious: An Emotional Justice Arts and Conversation* series in New York. A global citizen, she now lives in Brooklyn, New York.

Dr. Vincent Harding

As one of the icons of the civil rights movement, activist and author Dr. Vincent Harding was a friend and colleague of Dr. Martin Luther King Jr. and worked with Coretta Scott King to establish the King Center in Atlanta, serving as its first director. A distinguished theologian and historian, he is the award-winning author of several books, including *There Is a River*, *Hope and History*, and *Martin Luther King: The Inconvenient Hero*. Harding was professor of religion and social transformation at Denver's Iliff School of Theology from 1981 until his retirement in 2004. In 1997, Dr. Harding and his wife Rosemarie founded Veterans of Hope, an initiative on religion, culture, and participatory democracy that emphasizes nonviolent and grassroot approaches to social change.

Van Jones

Van Jones is an award-winning pioneer in human rights and the clean-energy economy. In 2011, he launched, with others, Rebuild the Dream, the hub of the American Dream Movement. Van is also a senior fellow at the Center for American Progress and a senior policy advisor at Green For All. At Princeton University, Jones holds a joint appointment as a distinguished visiting fellow in both the Center for African American Studies and in the Program in Science, Technology and Environmental Policy at the Woodrow Wilson School of Public and International Affairs. In 2009, Van Jones served as the green jobs adviser in the Obama White House and is the best-selling author of the definitive book on green jobs, *The Green Collar Economy*.

Dr. Julianne Malveaux

As the fifteenth president of Bennett College, Dr. Julianne Malveaux has been the architect of exciting and innovative transformation at America's oldest historically black college for women. Dr. Malveaux has long been recognized for her progressive and insightful observations. She is a labor economist, noted author, and colorful commentator.

Dr. Malveaux's popular writing has appeared in *USA Today*, *Black Issues in Higher Education*, *Ms. Magazine*, *Essence*, and the *Progressive*. Julianne Malveaux has been described by Dr. Cornel West as "the most iconoclastic public intellectual in the country." Her contributions to the public dialogue on issues such as race, culture, gender, and their economic impacts are shaping public opinion in twenty-first-century America.

Linn Washington Jr.

Linn Washington Jr. is a journalist and journalism professor. He writes a weekly column for the *Philadelphia Tribune* focused primarily on social justice issues. Washington is a cofounder of the online newspaper *This Can't Be Happening*—where he writes regularly on topics involving the news media, the criminal justice system, and racism. Washington has won many awards for investigative reporting and editorial writing during his journalism career spanning three-plus decades. As an associate professor of journalism at Temple University, Washington codirects the award-winning *Philadelphia Neighborhoods.com*, a local news Web site featuring multimedia content from urban communities. Washington is a graduate of the Yale Law Journalism Fellowship Program. He holds a BS in Communications from Temple University and a Masters in the Study of Law from the Yale Law School.